TO BE LIKE
JESUS

Studies in the Fruit of the Spirit

PAUL YOUNG

TO BE LIKE JESUS

Studies in the Fruit of the Spirit

TO BE LIKE JESUS: STUDIES IN THE FRUIT OF THE SPIRIT
By: Paul Young
Copyright © 2015
GOSPEL FOLIO PRESS
All Rights Reserved

Published by Gospel Folio Press
304 Killaly St. West Port Colborne, ON L3K 6A6

ISBN: 9781927521762

Cover design by Danielle Robins

Printed in Canada

Preface

Many years ago I led the morning Bible studies with a team of people (young and not so young) on an evangelistic mission in the Welsh industrial valleys. Each morning I was expected to speak and then discussion would follow. I chose for those studies the "Fruit of the Spirit". I felt inspired and deeply challenged as I studied them. They were certainly a blessing to my soul and others also expressed appreciation for the messages. Since then I have preached through the "Fruit of the Spirit" in a number of places and also done a series of radio talks on them.

I have now been asked to put them into a more permanent form and my thanks to all who have encouraged me to put the messages into a structure that is fit for publication. My prayer is that many more will be challenged, blessed and encouraged through a study of the multi-faceted diamond we call the "Fruit of the Spirit". The "Fruit of the Spirit" is about character and for the Christian the aim is to be like Christ. We are here on earth to become more like Christ, wonderfully in heaven we shall be like Him.   *Paul Young*

Introduction

A PARABLE FROM ANCIENT TIMES

The oldest parable in the Bible and many think in human history is found in the Old Testament book of Judges (Judg. 9:7-15). It is given by Jotham who was a son of the famous warrior-judge, Gideon, who had delivered Israel from foreign oppression and was their leader for 40 years. Gideon had fathered 70 sons but one of them was the son of a concubine from Shechem. His name was Abimelech. In an act of shameless treachery after the death of his father he killed all of Gideon's sons with one exception and that was the youngest son, Jotham. Abimelech made himself king of Shechem but as the ceremony was taking place Jotham stood on Mount Gerizim and shouted down the parable.

He said that the trees of the field were looking for a king. They asked the olive tree to be king but it refused to leave its natural work of producing olive oil. So the trees went to the fig tree but it also refused to be king and instead continued in its normal work of producing figs. Then they approached the vine but it also said, "No" as it did not want to leave its God-given task of producing grapes for wine. So they eventually went to the bramble.

Clearly there was a localized meaning to the parable that had application for Abimelech and the people of Shechem but it also reminds us that the function of trees is not to rule but to bear fruit. In a similar way we must focus not upon our authority but our usefulness to others and to the Lord's work. Bearing the fruit of good works, virtues and graces is paramount for every Christian, as children of God that is our aim and objective in life.

VARIOUS FRUIT

The New Testament, and indeed the Bible generally, lays a great deal of emphasis upon Christian fruitfulness. Indeed Jesus says that we can recognize true Christians from those who are false by their fruit. He said, *"By their fruit you will recognize them"* (Matt. 7:16, 20, NIV). So this is an important subject with strong implications for us today. The New Testament gives a range of fruitfulness that ought to be seen in Christian believers.

A. **THE FRUIT OF CONVERTS**: Jesus told the parable of the Sower (Mark 4) and it is a picture of the true Christian scattering the seeds of the gospel. It simply means that we share the truth of gospel with those who need to hear it. Some will instantly forget, others will seem to embrace the message but will not be really committed, but others will sincerely accept the message. It will take root in their lives and they will truly be converted to Christ. It is a glorious blessing to lead others to saving faith in Christ and that is the wonderful fruit that flows from our personal evangelism. It can be costly in time, energy and prayer but it is eternally worth it. The Old Testament psalmist put it this way, *"He that goeth forth and weepeth, bearing precious seed, shall doubtless come again with rejoicing, bringing his sheaves with him"* (Ps. 126:6).

B. **THE FRUIT OF PRAISE**: this is deep appreciation to God, from our hearts, for His many wonderful blessings and mercies. Most of all it is thanksgiving and praise for the transcendent gift of His Son, Jesus Christ. The writer of the book of Hebrews put it this way, *"Through Jesus, therefore, let us continually offer to God a sacrifice of praise - the fruit of lips that confess his name"* (Heb. 13:15, NIV). We notice that Christians should be continually in an attitude of praise and giving expressions of worth to God. Also it is a *"sacrifice"* and that involves giving up in order to praise

8

and certainly it requires time and energy, as well as personal discipline. We don't always feel like praising the Lord but it is at those times that the reality of our fruitfulness is revealed.

C. THE FRUIT OF CHARACTER: this is known as the fruit of the Spirit and is mentioned in Galatians 5:22-23. Nine characteristics are mentioned and all need to be developed within the life of the Christian. When these are rooted in a Christian they produce a Christlike character and so the aim of all true believers in the Saviour should be to live and be like our Lord. We will try to develop an understanding of these characteristics as we unfold the truth of the fruit of the Spirit.

THE HOLY SPIRIT

We notice that this fruit is *"of the Spirit"* but in many Christian circles there have been deep debates regarding the person and work of the Holy Spirit. Certainly the Holy Spirit is a person and yet at the same time is deity. Thus, as the third member of the Trinity, He is God. Also the Holy Spirit indwells every Christian. This fact is made clear in the following verses, *"You, however, are controlled not by the sinful nature but by the Spirit, if the Spirit of God lives in you. And if anyone does not have the Spirit of Christ, he does not belong to Christ"* (Rom. 8:9, NIV). Again we read, *"Because you are sons, God sent the Spirit of his Son into our hearts, the Spirit who calls out, 'Abba, Father'"* (Gal. 4:6, NIV).

It is important to remember that every action of the Spirit is in accordance with His character which is holy and that is why He is called the Holy Spirit. Also, all His activities are in accordance with the Word of God and ultimately for the glory of the Saviour, the Lord Jesus. Indeed Jesus says of the Spirit, *"He will bring glory to me"* (John 16:14, NIV). So the fruit of the Spirit in the lives of Christians should bring glory to the name of Christ.

There has been a lot of emphasis among Christians upon the **gifts** of the Spirit, often with a majoring upon the more spectacular gifts. However, there has tended to be much less emphasis upon "the **fruit** of the Spirit". Certainly no one has all the gifts of the Spirit and we are not responsible for receiving those gifts, as is made clear in 1 Corinthians 12:7-11. However we are responsible for recognizing our gifts and using them for the glory of the Lord. Yet if there was more focus upon the fruit of the Spirit then there would be fewer problems in churches today.

Many years ago I did a year's study on the Holy Spirit with my Bible class of thirty Christian teenagers. Right at the end I brought a focus upon "the fruit of the Spirit". In many ways I regretted leaving it until the last part of the study as I came to realize the importance of the subject.

ONLY ONE FRUIT

When we read the phrase *"fruit of the Spirit"* we must remember that in that context of Galatians 5:22-23 the word *"fruit"* is a singular word. I know that the word can be used in English in either a singular or plural manner but Paul used it to emphasize that there is only one fruit of the Spirit and yet he then gives a list of nine characteristics. Certainly this draws our attention to two factors.

A. There is only one *source or origin* for these nine characteristics that are designated as *"fruit of the Spirit"*. That source is the Holy Spirit. Thus the Lord Himself through the operation of the Holy Spirit supernaturally produces the fruit in the lives of Christian believers. Therefore these characteristics cannot be worked up by human ingenuity or effort but are ultimately the work of God's Spirit in our lives.

B. The use of the singular word *"fruit"* reminds us that the sole fruit is "love". The nine-fold fruit of the Spirit is all an expression of love. The other eight all flow from the wonder of love. Thus if we love someone we are joyful with them, at peace with them, have patience with them, are gentle with them and so on. I suppose the best way to look at the fruit of the Spirit is to imagine it as a beautiful diamond with many faces. The diamond glints differently as it moves and its beauty is variable depending upon the angle with which one sees it. So the fruit of the Spirit can be viewed from nine different angles and each one is an expression of the beauty of the Lord Jesus in the life of the Christian.

HOW CAN WE BE FRUITFUL FOR GOD?

1. THERE IS NEED TO REMAIN OR ABIDE IN CHRIST.

The Lord Jesus said, *"Remain in me, and I will remain in you. No branch can bear fruit by itself; it must remain in the vine. Neither can you bear fruit unless you remain in me. I am the vine; you are the branches. If a man remains in me and I in him, he will bear much fruit; apart from me you can do nothing"* (John 15:4-5, NIV). The rather obvious truth is that a branch of a vine cannot bear fruit by itself. If we cut a branch off the tree and place it on the ground it will never produce any fruit. It is only as the branch is deeply imbedded in the tree that fruit appears upon it. Thus the branch does not produce the fruit, it only bears the fruit. It is the goodness that flows from the tree to the branch that enables fruit to be produced. Clearly the picture is that Christ is the vine and individual Christians are the branches. We have no ability by ourselves to produce fruit and can only bear fruit as we are deeply imbedded in the Lord Jesus. That simply means that we have received Christ as our Saviour and subsequently are willing to enthrone Him as Lord and Master of our lives; it is being obedient to Him in all parts of life and having a deepening experience of fellowship with the Saviour. It is only as we are willing to deny sin and yield to the authority and leading of the Lord in our lives that we will be seen to bear the fruit of the Spirit.

2. THERE IS NEED TO REMAIN IN THE WORD OF GOD

In Psalm 1 we read, *"But his delight is in the law of the LORD, and on his law he meditates day and night. He is like a tree planted by streams of water, which yields its fruit in season and whose leaf does not wither. Whatever he does prospers"* (vv. 2-3, NIV). Again the focus is upon trees. It is the tree planted by a river of water. Such a tree is constantly and bounteously fruitful, because it is never short of moisture to sustain it. The Bible referred to in these verses as *"the law of the LORD"* is the equivalent of that river for the Christian. To be spiritually fruitful the Christian has to be constantly "drinking" at the fountain of the Word of God. This is so important for every believer in Christ.

Firstly the Word of God has a cleansing effect upon our minds and hearts. There is so much bombarding our minds today of a negative, unclean and polluting nature that it is even more important to focus upon the Word of God. This will help us to live clean, holy and spiritually healthy lives that show the fruit of character, namely the fruit of the Spirit.

The story is told of a young man who became a Christian. Every day he read a chapter of Scripture but seemed to understand very little of what he read and retained even less in his mind. After a while he became very discouraged and so went to one of his church elders with the problem. He explained that it was hardly worthwhile to read the Bible because he understood and remembered so little. The elder encouraged him to continue reading the Word of God, but didn't have much success until he told him about a sieve. He asked what would be the point of filling a sieve with water. The young man said, "No point, as the water flows through it", but he could see a point to the question that his own mind was a bit like the sieve in that what he read seemed to go straight through it! However, the elder pointed out that there was one particular use for pouring water into a sieve and that is to keep the sieve clean!

Introduction

A missionary in China who was imprisoned by the Japanese during World War II, managed to take a forbidden gospel of John with her into prison. She carefully hid it, and each night when she went to bed, she pulled the covers over her head and memorized one verse. She did this until the day she was freed. When the prisoners were released, most of them shuffled out, but the missionary was so chipper someone said she must have been brainwashed. A *Life* magazine reporter who had interviewed her said, "She's been brainwashed for sure, God washed her brain"[1].

So it is important to constantly read the Bible to maintain cleanness in our minds, lives and behaviour. This was what the Psalmist meant when he wrote, *"I have hidden your word in my heart that I might not sin against you"* (Ps. 119:11, NIV). So we must remain in the Word of God for daily cleansing of our lives and it also helps us to conquer temptation and to resist the Devil's intrigues. Thus to experience the joy of the fruitfulness of holiness we must remain in the Word of God through regular and faithful reading of the Bible.

Secondly, we need to fill our minds with the Word of God if we are ever to be effective in personal evangelism. If we are to lead people to Christ and salvation it is never going to be simply our arguments, force of personality or cleverness, but it is as we use the Word of God effectively and under the leading of the Holy Spirit. That is why the writer of Hebrews says, *"For the word of God is living and active. Sharper than any double-edged sword, it penetrates even to dividing soul and spirit, joints and marrow; it judges the thoughts and attitudes of the heart"* (Heb. 4:12, NIV). Stephen Olford underlines this particular point in his book, *The Secret of Soul Winning.* "The soul winner will be hampered again and again if his memory is not well stored with passages from the Word of God that are likely to be of use to him in leading men and women to a personal knowledge of Christ."[2] So if we are ever to experi-

---

1   Billy Graham, Hope for Each Day: Morning and Evening Devotions, (Nashville: Thomas Nelson, 2002), 597.

2   Stephen Olford, *The Secret of Soul Winning,* (Nashville: B&H Publishing Group: 2007), 34-35.

ence the joy of fruitfulness in terms of converts to Christ then we must remain in the Word of God.

Thirdly, when our minds and hearts are filled with the Word of God then we are able to worship the Lord more fully. We are enabled both in our personal, private lives and in our corporate life as a church to be enriched in worship when we are seeped in the Word of God. Certainly as we take the psalms, which are very much expressions of praise to God, and make them our own then we can worship God in fullness using the very words of Scripture. So we need to remain in the Word of God if we are to experience the joy of fruitfulness in terms of praise to God.

So as we remain in Christ and in His Word we can know the blessing of bearing fruit for His glory.

THE FRUIT THE SPIRIT IS SEEN IN CLUSTERS

Natural fruit growing on fruit trees is often produced in clusters such as grapes. So as we look at the fruit of the Spirit we can divide it into three clusters as follows.

A. THE GODWARD CLUSTER: here we see three aspects of the fruit of the Spirit in terms of our direct relationship with God. So we see this first group as love, joy and peace. Thus we read of the *"love...of God"* (1 John 4:7), *"rejoice* (joy) *in the Lord"* (Phil. 3:1) and of the *"peace of God"* (Phil. 4:7). This cluster particularly highlights aspects of God's character that need to be seen in Christians. We should be loving, joyful and peaceable.

B. THE OUTWARD OR MANWARD CLUSTER: here we see three characteristics of the fruit of the Spirit in terms of our relationship with other people. Thus we are reminded that with people we should be patient, gentle and good. These are the very characteristics that allow for good human relationships and enriching social contacts. They enable the development of true Christian fellowship and overcome many problems and irritants that can arise between people.

C. THE INWARD CLUSTER: here we see three aspects of the fruit of the Spirit in terms of our inward selves. We should be faithful, meek and self-controlled (temperate).

We must not push these divisions too far and we are well aware that they overlap with each other and are not exclusive compartments. Certainly they all have to do with inward characteristics of the Christian, they all affect our relationships with other people and they all reflect our relationship with the Lord.

We can also say that the fruit of the Spirit was most fully and most wonderfully witnessed in the life of the Lord Jesus. He lived out the fruit of the Spirit in absolute fullness. He was the most loving and compassionate person ever to walk on this earth. He overflowed with joy and peace. He was the most patient of people and constantly showed kindness as a reflection of His wonderful and wholesome goodness. He was utterly faithful especially to His Father and was always gentle and self-controlled. He is our example of someone who truly lived the fruit of the Spirit. We are called to walk in His footsteps, to be like Him and to show the nine-fold fruit of the Spirit in our lives as Christians.

1

True Love

The supreme happiness in life is the conviction
that we are loved.   Victor Hugo

"The fruit of the Spirit is love…" (Gal. 5:22, NIV). This is
a most wonderful statement and simply says that when the
Spirit of God works in someone's life then the result is that he
or she becomes deeply loving towards others. I well remember the times I used to visit an ex-prisoner who was trying to
recover from the traumas of his crime and prison life. He was
deeply interested in the gospel and was reading Christian
books. He asked me one day why one particular author
kept using the word "a gap". Of course when we looked at
the word it was the Greek word for love "agape". He won-
dered why the author didn't simply use the word "love". So
I explained that there are various words in Greek that mean
love and this was the highest form of love, higher than the
love between husband and wife, between parents and children or between friends. This is a beautiful word that genuinely wants the best for someone else, even if that involves
great personal sacrifice to give the best.

This is the great characteristic of God, who is the God of
love, even to those who do not deserve His love. This love
was revealed on earth when Jesus died for our sins on the
cross. He sacrificed Himself so that we might have the great
gift of salvation. No wonder the Bible says, *"But you, O Lord,
are a compassionate…God…abounding in love…"* (Ps. 86:15,
NIV). This love is the most wonderful force in the universe
and I trust that we have experienced its blessing in our lives.
It must never be confused with lust or self-gratification. There

is nothing selfish about this love and is developed in the Christian by the work of the Holy Spirit.

As a student it was my privilege to meet a Christian gentleman who with his friend had, in their younger days, evangelized a great area of Mid Wales. I along with others listened in awed and fascinated silence to what he had to say and he concluded by saying, "If you don't love the people then it is a waste of time". That statement has stayed with me and is certainly true, for we remember that in the parable that Jesus told in Luke 10, that the Good Samaritan "took pity" or "had compassion" upon the man who had been attacked and robbed and left for dead on the side of the road. He showed love to that man, a love that moved him to action and took real practical form in terms of medicine, sustenance and a bed for the night. True love must find practical expression.

The greatest example of such love, as we have indicated, is the Lord Jesus. He demonstrated the true love of God by showing compassion to the great crowds that followed Him and He fed them. He showed compassion to the children who flocked to be near Him. He loved the disciples and people sensed the deep love He had for them. Yet the love of Christ was finally and fully realized at Calvary when He died for the sins of mankind. His love was not *"...with words or tongue but with actions and in truth"* (1 John 3:18, NIV). This was the glorious expression of God's love for us as we read, *"This is love: not that we loved God, but that he loved us and sent his Son as an atoning sacrifice for our sins...since God so loved us, we also ought to love one another"* (1 John 4:10-11, NIV). Such love is not simply an emotion or a feeling but a commitment to action for the benefit of others and that was certainly true of the Saviour's love for us.

That love must be seen in our lives as Christian people and if it is absent then people have the right to question whether we are truly Christian.

HOW IS THIS LOVE SEEN?

The Lord Jesus instructed His followers to love one another *"as I have loved you"* (John 13:34). This is the key to understanding how this love should be demonstrated amongst Christian people. We can say three things.

A. HE LOVED US AS HE FOUND US: that is quite incredible. He did not wait for us to improve a little bit or to get rid of some of our more sinful and irritating practices. He simply loved us as He found us with all our sins, failures, selfish attitudes and lustful thoughts. In the same way we must demonstrate the same loving loyalty to fellow believers in Christ. We must love them as we find them. They may at times be difficult, insensitive and ungracious but that is no excuse for not loving them, remembering that love is the willingness to do the very best for them.

B. HE LOVED US IN A PRACTICAL WAY: He went all the way to Calvary and paid the price for our sin by dying in agony and shame on the cross. Jesus did not simply stand in heaven and tell us that He loved us. He demonstrated that love in the most wonderful and practical manner. Similarly as Christian people we are not called to simply talk about love but to show it. So negatively we will never do or say anything bad about another fellow Christian and positively we will do all we can to help, support and advise them, even if this involves great inconvenience to ourselves.

I received a telephone call at 2:30 a.m. after a long day of travel and ministry. The voice was one of the older young people in our youth group. The temperature was at freezing point and he was huddled on a bench in the town centre. His mother had locked the house doors (inadvertently) and he was unable to rouse her when he got back late from babysitting. He needed help and needed it at that moment. I brought him home, my wife had made up the spare bed and he had a warm, good night's sleep. It was inconvenient but the call of God to help people must be heeded and never ignored.

C. **HE LOVED EVERYONE:** the Lord died on the cross as an atonement for the sins of the world. It was inclusive love and the salvation gained on Calvary is available to everyone and simply needs to be accepted in faith. Similarly our love should be inclusive and no Christian should be excluded from the orbit of our love. We need to embrace all with our love, even if they are in a different age group from ourselves, a different social background, a different culture, racial or national background or even with a different intellectual ability. There should be a wonderful unity and wholeness engendered by the deep love of Christ in our hearts.

Yet this love is much more embracing than simply those who are fellow Christians. We are called to love all people, whoever they may be. With deep sensitivity, prayerfulness and real concern we should try to meet need wherever we may find it, even to those who may be our enemies. One thinks of the lady whose husband left her for an adulterous relationship. Eventually through the tears and pain she was able to go to that other lady and give her a gift, a bouquet of roses and say, "Because of Christ's love for me and through me I can love you". That is quite amazing but it is the reality of God's love in us.

Bishop Festo Kevingere was a church leader in Uganda during the brutal regime of Idi Amin when so many Christians were killed in the most horrific circumstances. Church leaders did not escape and friends of the bishop were also killed by Amin's soldiers but he wrote, "My hardness and bitterness towards those who were persecuting us could only bring spiritual loss. This would take away my ability to communicate the love of God, which is the essence of my ministry and my testimony. So I had to ask forgiveness from the Lord and for grace to love President Amin more…This was fresh air for my tired soul. I knew I had seen the Lord and had been released: love filled my heart"[3].

This reminds us that Christianity is about love, namely Christ loving us and filling our hearts with His love by His Spirit. This was the love that burned in the hearts of the first century Christian believers and caused them to be motivated to go to an antagonistic world and bring the gospel of Jesus Christ to the people. This needs to be the motive, namely love that should drive Christians in all they do. This love should firstly be love for God, secondly for fellow Christians and thirdly for all people, whoever they may be.

HOW CAN THIS LOVE DEVELOP IN OUR LIVES?

Let us consider a number of approaches to answering this crucial question.

A. **RESPONSE:** we love the Lord because He first loved us. It is our response to the initiative that God made to us in Christ. There has to be a deep and real relationship between seeing and loving. For example I never loved my wife before I saw her. In seeing her I fell in love with her. The Lord Jesus looked at the rich young ruler and it says, *"Jesus looked at him and loved him"* (Mark 10:21, NIV). As we gain a clear glimpse of our Lord and Saviour, Jesus Christ then we start to love Him. One writer said that at the age of fifteen he started to read Mark's gospel, as he did, "God revealed His Son to me, with the inner eye I saw Jesus. That was when I began to love Him."

This is not an act of will but a Spirit-inspired response to the God who reveals Himself to us in Christ. Thus the more we look, the more we love and so we need

---

3   Festo Kevingere, *I Love Idi Amin: The Story of Triumph under Fire in the Midst of Suffering and Persecution in Uganda,* (Ada: Fleming H. Revell Company, 1977)

to keep on seeing the Saviour through reading and meditating upon the Holy Bible and then we will keep loving the Lord as we should and that love will flow through us to others as we help meet their need.

B. INDEBTEDNESS: the intensity of a person's love for God is dependent upon the depth of his experience of forgiveness. This is exactly what Jesus said about a particular woman who showed Him very great devotion. He said, *"Wherefore I say unto thee, Her sins, which are many, are forgiven; for she loved much: but to whom little is forgiven, the same loveth little"* (Luke 7:47). Thus true love springs from the gratitude we feel to Christ for deliverance from sin and its penalty. Sometimes that sense of gratitude can be overwhelming. This was true of the aged John Newton, one time captain of a slave ship and a blasphemer. He said, "My memory is nearly gone, but I remember two things, that I am a great sinner and that Jesus is a great Saviour." It is seeing these two things together that enables our love to increase and deepen. A sense of indebtedness leads to a fuller sense of gratitude and a greater love for the Saviour.

C. PRESENCE: it is often said, "that absence makes the heart grow fonder". There is a certain amount of truth in that but is only really true if absences are alternated with being together on a regular basis. It would appear to be more true to say, "that out of sight is out of mind". Clearly love grows between people when they live, work and share together. This is the same with God. The more we are found in His presence then the more we love Him. This not only applies to church meetings or fellowship times but we need to be constantly meditating upon the Lord and His Word and recollecting the blessings that He bestows. It is the discipline of making our mind focus upon the truth of Scripture and habitually turning our attention to the Lord. Eventually the conscience effort will become unconscious enjoyment. I well remember learning this lesson as a student when I once met an older Christian as I strolled along the road. He simply mentioned the fact that as he was walking his thoughts were dwelling upon the verse from Job 19:25 that said, *"I know that my Redeemer lives"* (NIV). I recognized that he had been blessed and also that we can grow in love for God by practising the presence of the Lord, through focusing our minds upon the words of Scripture.

D. FELLOWSHIP: the fruit of the Spirit is not produced in isolation but in fellowship with others, especially fellow Christians in the local church. The local church is really the school where we are taught to truly love one another. This is the idea behind the words of the writer of Hebrews, *"And let us consider one another to provoke unto love and to good works: Not forsaking the assembling of ourselves together, as the manner of some is; but exhorting one another: and so much the more, as ye see the day approaching"* (Heb. 10:24-25). Certainly it is true that "we can meet without loving, but we cannot love without meeting". It is possible to be in church services where there is no love and everything is simply cold, formal and uninspiring. However, to show real love we have to meet with others and in the context of personal relationships true love is revealed and developed. Thus love comes to genuine and glorious maturity in a local community of Christians who truly want to reflect the character of Christ.

E. CREATION: as we view the wonder of the world and the universe around us we are struck by the awesomeness of God who created it all. As we see it we are struck by the majesty of God and in comparison we are so small and insignificant and yet we delight in the fact that we are recipients of His deep love and we are caused to love Him in response. I grew up on a farm in South Wales and it was a delight to walk alone in the woods on the mountains and be alone with God. There was an awesome sense of God and a depth of fellowship and love for the Saviour that was deeply felt. It was the same when I was a student in university on the coast. I used to look out at night-time at the great ocean and it produced a deep awareness of God and a response of love toward Him.

F. **ACTION:** it is true that love grows by action. We therefore need to practice love to keep it alive and growing. This was what the church at Thessalonica were doing as Paul makes clear, *"Now about brotherly love we do not need to write to you, for you yourselves have been taught by God to love each other. And in fact, you do love all the brothers throughout Macedonia. Yet we urge you, brothers, to do so more and more"* (1 Thess. 4:9-10, NIV). The idea of *"brotherly love"* is the love that children of the same father should show towards each other. It is really another term for Christian love. All Christians have entered into God's family through faith in Christ and so have become children of God. Thus there should be a special bond of love between those who are children of God. Certainly Paul was encouraged with the Thessalonian Christians who were showing deep, compassionate love for each other in the city and also for all the Christians in the province of Macedonia. Yet Paul calls for an increase even in their demonstration of love. The only limits upon love in action are the opportunities for doing it. Clearly if no such opportunity arises then we can't show love, but whenever such a need arises we must demonstrate the fruit of the Spirit which is love.

The call to Christians is to show on-going love. A love that is not slushy sentimentality but is practical, love in action. This has to be our motivation because if we *"have not love, I (we) gain nothing"* (1 Cor. 13:3, NIV). Without love then all our activity and occupation for the Lord is worthless, vain, useless and empty. Indeed, *"love never fails"* (1 Cor. 13:8, NIV). This is the abiding principle as the apostle Paul wrote, *"And now these three remain: faith, hope and love. But the greatest of these is love"* (1 Cor. 13:13, NIV). So above all else we, as Christians should be motivated and governed by love. Love should characterize us and we should be known for our loving, compassionate attitude and for our willingness to meet the needs of others with practical loving concern.

I talked with a Christian from North America who, with his wife, had walked across Northern England from coast to coast. They stayed at various bed and breakfast places along the way and their luggage was forwarded each day to the next stopping point. They linked up with others as they walked who were doing the same tour. One Sunday evening they decided to attend a gospel chapel in the village, while the others preferred a service in the local Anglican Church. In the chapel they had a wonderful welcome, had tea and cakes after the service and came away deeply blessed by the loving time of Christian fellowship. The others had attended the service where no one acknowledged them, there were no words of welcome and having sat through a cold, formal service they left with no sense of warmth or expression of love. They felt they had been ignored and wished they had attended the chapel. True love is a wonderful blessing. We must make sure that we show it and share it for the glory of Jesus Christ.

> People need love, especially when they don't deserve it.

Wonderful Joy

There is a marvellous medicinal power in joy…
C. H. Spurgeon

"The fruit of the Spirit is…joy" (Gal. 5:22, NIV) and joy should be a genuine characteristic of the true Christian. Essentially it is a deep gladness in the heart and is an ability to praise God no matter what the circumstances and problems of life may be. Thus this joy is spiritual and is certainly not something that we could ever work up by ourselves. Its source is divine and supernatural, namely the Holy Spirit and it is revealed in our lives in proportion to our obedience and submission to the Lordship of Christ. This is joy despite the circumstances we go through.

There was a missionary family serving the Lord in an Asian country a long time ago. During their time in that nation thy lost an infant son and had to conduct a funeral in a windswept cemetery. They arrived back to their home and the father sat down and wrote to family and friends in the United States and he said "When we came back from the funeral there were tears in our eyes but joy in our hearts". Clearly he did not minimize the trauma of losing a young son but in the will of God he had found the joy of the Lord. Circumstances had not taken away their deep spiritual joy.

Years ago a journalist went around the various churches of his town to write articles about their services. At one church there were a couple walking ahead of him holding the hands of their young son as they went into the building. The son caught his shin on the steps and started to cry. The Dad looked down at his son and said, "Son, say 'Hallelujah'". The boy managed to do this despite his tears and the journalist was very impressed and wrote, "Give me a religion that says, 'Hallelujah' through the tears!" That is exactly Christianity because we can rejoice despite the many adverse circumstances of life.

The words "joy" and "happiness" are often used interchangeably but joy is not the same thing as happiness because happiness is very much external and very shallow. Happiness is based upon favourable happenings in my life and when things go well I can be happy, but inevitably there will come times when matters are less favourable and I will lose my happiness. "Happiness is an emotion, and joy is an attitude. Emotions come and go, but attitudes come and grow"[4]. "Don't confuse happiness with joy. Happiness comes with happy circumstances; joy wells up deep inside our souls as we learn to trust Christ. Joy does not mean that we are never sad or that we never cry. But joy is a quiet confidence, a state of inner peace that comes from God. Life's troubles may rob us of our happiness, but they can never rob us of the joy God gives us, as we turn in faith to Him and seek His face"[5]. Neither is joy the same as pleasure because that is a most fleeting and momentary experience. It soon passes whereas joy is lasting. Joy is something different from both happiness and pleasure.

Joy is a God-given quality that is mediated through His Holy Spirit. It is a characteristic available to Christians despite unfavourable conditions and is lasting. The missionaries Paul and Silas were arrested in the city of Philippi and were severely flogged and then placed in stocks in the innermost prison cell. We can imagine them in pain, in darkness, in discomfort and to say their circumstances were unfavourable is the least of it. Yet they were not robbed of joy and were able to sing praise to God and engage in prayer. It was also true of the Christians at Thessalonica who had received the Word of God in much affliction but *with joy of the Holy Ghost* (1

---

4   Robert J. Morgan
5   Billy Graham, *Hope for Each Day: Morning and Evening Devotions*, (Tennessee: Thomas Nelson, 2002), 644

Thess. 1:6). As new converts to Christ they had immediately faced affliction, persecution and distressing circumstances, as well as seeing their founder, the apostle Paul being expelled from their city. Yet they had been sustained by spiritual joy engendered by the Holy Spirit and had found the words of the Old Testament leader Nehemiah to be true, *"The joy of the Lord is your strength"* (Neh. 8:10). So joy is not superficial, passing or natural but supernatural and results from our relationship with the Lord. The deeper that relationship gets, the greater the joy.

THE EPISTLE OF JOY

The letter that Paul wrote to the church at Philippi has sometimes been called the "epistle of joy" because a dominant theme is that of joy and rejoicing. The key verse is, *"Rejoice in the Lord always, I will say it again: Rejoice!"* (Phil. 4:4, NIV). The words "joy" or "rejoice" occur 16 times in the epistle and are found every chapter. Clearly Paul wanted the Philippian believers to be absolutely sure that no matter what happened to them they were to rejoice continually. In the epistle joy is seen in three areas of spiritual life. Firstly, in the Christian's devotional life; secondly, in the Christian's service and thirdly in the Christian's relationships with other believers in Christ.

1. JOY IN THE CHRISTIAN'S DEVOTIONAL LIFE

The apostle Paul highlights this in three ways.

A. IN PRAYER

"In all my prayers for all of you, I always pray with joy" (Phil. 1:4, NIV). The prayer life of a Christian believer should be characterized by joy. Yet so often we find prayer to be hard work and the need for discipline and effort seems too much. Indeed the sheer hard work of prayer can rob us of joy and

make our prayer time a terrible drudgery. The true joy of prayer is harnessed to discipline and we need to pray that the barriers of sin in our lives will be broken and the joy of Christ would flood our souls.

Also as we focus upon our Saviour in prayer our hearts can be uplifted and we can rejoice in the glory of the One who loved us and died for our sins on the cross. As we pray for fellow believers they can often bring us joy as we remember the blessing that they are to us. Also as we pray of those who as yet are unsaved we can rejoice that when the Lord answers our prayers and saves them they too will rejoice with us. We remember that in the Old Testament when Moses, the servant of God, had communed with the Lord on the mountain his face shone with the reflected glory of God. As we spend time with the Lord in prayer then our spiritual faces will shine with that reflected glory and what joy that gives to the Christian.

Truly it can be said, "no prayer, no joy". A prayerless Christian soon becomes a joyless Christian because joy flows from our relationship with God that deepens as we engage in true prayerfulness.

So Paul found joy in prayer and so can we.

B. IN FAITH

"Convinced of this, I know that I will remain, and I will continue with all of you for your progress and joy in the faith" (Phil. 1:25, NIV). A life of faith engenders deep joy. When we have heard the voice of God and have stepped out in faith to obey the word of the Lord and taken the opportunity to serve Him, then we have experienced deep joy. Years ago a lady told me that on one New Year's morning as she was having her quiet time the Lord directed her thoughts to the next door neighbours. As she continued praying she sensed that she needed to go round and wish them a Happy New Year. This certainly surprised her husband when she told him what she was about to do. He pointed out that in the six years the

neighbours had lived next door she had never done such a thing before! However she felt constrained by the Lord to do it and so with some trepidation she went next door and wished the man when he opened the door a happy new year and said that she was praying for him and his wife. To her amazement the man opened the door wide and asked her in and there was his wife in tears. He said, "My wife faces a serious operation in the next few days and we have just asked the question, 'Who can we turn to?' and you have come round to say you will pray for us". It gave her joy to take an opportunity to talk about the one person, the Lord Jesus who could be relied upon to help them and they needed to trust Him as their Saviour. She had deep joy in responding to the Lord's leading and then in faith to serve Him.

Our hearts are also warmed with joy as we read of the great examples of faith such as those recorded in Hebrews 11. Also those who went out on missionary service dependent in faith upon the Lord inspire us. Men such as William Carey to India, George Muller in Bristol, the five martyrs in Ecuador, Hudson Taylor in China, David Livingstone in Africa or James Gilmour to Mongolia. Yet even today God's people still exercise faith as they do the work of evangelism and the result is true joyfulness.

So Paul found joy in Christian faith.

C. IN THE LORD

"Rejoice in the Lord" (Phil. 3:1; 4:4, NIV). The apostle makes it clear that such joy is only found in Christ. So to experience this wonderful joy a person needs to know Christ as Saviour. However, it does say, *"in the Lord"* and not simply "in Christ". The difference is that *"in the Lord"* means a total devotion in obedience to the Saviour. So it isn't enough to get rid of surface sins but also deep-rooted rebellion in our hearts must be driven out. The root of sinfulness as well as the fruit of sin must be removed so that our lives become obedient to the will of the Lord. To know God's purpose for our lives and fulfill it,

this is the secret of true joyfulness. In the will of God is my joy. In the words of the famous hymn: "All to Jesus I surrender"[6] .

So Paul found joy in the Lord.

2. JOY IN THE CHRISTIAN'S SERVICE

The joy of the Lord is found in activity for God through engaging in the work that the Lord has called and equipped us to perform. Again Paul sees this in three ways.

A. IN PROCLAIMING THE GOSPEL

"But what does it matter? The important thing is that in every way, whether from false motives or true, Christ is preached. And because of this I rejoice" (Phil. 1:18, NIV). Paul was in a prison cell in Rome writing this epistle but he knew that some people were preaching the gospel because of the goodwill they felt towards him. However others preached out of envy and rivalry. This did not discourage him because he simply rejoiced that the message of salvation was being proclaimed. It warms our hearts and brings joy to our souls to hear the message of the gospel proclaimed. It might not be by people in our particular circle but that should not stop us delighting whenever the message is heard.

So Paul found joy in gospel proclamation.

B. IN MARTYRDOM

"But even if I am being poured out like a drink offering on the sacrifice and service coming from your faith, I am glad and rejoice with all of you. So you should be glad and rejoice with me" (Phil. 2:17-18, NIV). We may find it hard to accept or understand that the apostle Paul rejoiced that he would be sacrificed as a martyr for his faith in Christ. He found it a joy to be identified with Christ in an unfair and unjust death and execution simply because he was a Christian. He appeared to have found

---

6   Judson W. Van de Venter, *I Surrender All*

cause for rejoicing in the fact that the Lord could entrust him to bear a good testimony in the face of martyrdom. Interestingly many in history who have lost their lives through martyrdom seem to have entered into death with great joy and it would be good to pray that the Lord would give us joy, so that we might be faithful even unto death. Also Paul anticipated the delight of seeing his Saviour's face as he contemplated death and that must have given him overwhelming joy.

The day James Guthrie was to be executed as a martyr for his faith, he woke up at 4:00 a.m. He took time to pray to God, read his Bible and worship the Lord, as he had done every day for years. When asked how he felt, he said, *"This is the day the Lord has made; let us rejoice and be glad in it"* (Ps. 118:24, NIV). In the Old Testament God's servant, Job said, *"Though he slay me, yet will I hope in him"* (Job 13:15, NIV).

So Paul found joy in the prospect of Christian martyrdom.

C. IN GIVING

"I rejoice greatly in the Lord that at last you have renewed your concern for me. Indeed, you have been concerned, but you had no opportunity to show it" (Phil. 4:10, NIV). Christian giving in terms of finance, hospitality and deep care results in wonderful joy both for the giver and the receiver. To know that we have fulfilled a pressing need by giving is a joyful experience. To have a pressing need met is also a joyful experience. The Philippians had helped meet the needs of the imprisoned apostle and it had given him immense joy.

3. JOY IN RELATIONSHIP WITH OTHER CHRISTIANS

Paul defines this in three ways.

A. IN UNITY

"Then make my joy complete by being like-minded, having the same love, being one in spirit and purpose" (Phil. 2:2, NIV). It

is always a delight and joy to see and experience the unity of God's people and it is always a tragedy and a grief when God's people are divided. It is only as God's people know true unity and oneness that God can truly bless and enrich their lives. So Paul saw joy in Christian oneness. The Psalmist wrote, *"Behold, how good and how pleasant it is for brethren to dwell together in unity"* (Ps. 133:1).

B. IN SPIRITUAL LEADERS

"Therefore I am…eager to send him (Epaphroditus), *so that when you see him again you may be glad…welcome him in the Lord with great joy, and honor men like him"* (Phil. 2:28-29, NIV). Epaphroditus was a great spiritual leader of the church in Philippi and brought joy both to the apostle and to the Philippian Christians. Such godly leaders, who lead by personal example and who are devoted to the Lord are a genuine source of joy to the Lord's people. They sacrificially serve the Lord and never count the cost. Such leaders are greatly needed today. Paul found joy in spiritual leaders.

C. IN SPIRITUAL CHILDREN

"…you whom I love and long for, my joy and crown…stand firm in the Lord" (Phil. 4:1, NIV). It is a very rich joy to have children in the Lord. To have led them to Christ and to see them grow into strong Christians is a great thrill and a deep joy. Paul had cause to rejoice in the fact that his spiritual children at Philippi were growing in the Lord.

Joy is seen in so many ways and it is worthwhile studying the book of Philippians in detail to gain a strong understanding of the subject of Christian joy. It needs to be remembered that true joy is a wonderful testimony of the power of Jesus Christ in this world in which we live, because that world is so often gloomy and depressed with many troubles, worries and fears. To see a joyful Christian who delights in Christ and who lives not with foolish laughter but with an ability to praise God no matter what circumstances he passes through is a glorious revelation of what the Lord can do in a human life. Someone has written,

> Just as all the water in the world cannot quench the Holy Spirit, neither can all the troubles and tragedies of the world overwhelm the joy which the Spirit brings into the human heart.
> *Billy Graham*

Ultimately the fullness of this joy is realized in God's presence in heaven. As we contemplate the wonder of heaven we can say with the apostle Peter, *"...though now ye see him not, yet believing, ye rejoice with joy unspeakable and full of glory: Receiving the end of your faith, even the salvation of your souls"* (1 Pet. 1:8-9). This anticipation should cause us to rejoice now and that is a prelude to the words of Paul, *"Rejoice evermore"* (1 Thess. 5:16). May joy be the hallmark of our lives as we live each day for Jesus Christ. May we live lives that honour and glorify our heavenly Father.

So joy is a petal of the flower of love and true love leads to wonderful joy. That joy is found in activity as we know God's will and complete it successfully and is also found in people—the true people of God whose hearts are knit with ours in service for the Lord. But ultimately the joy of our hearts is when we see the Lord: *"Then were the disciples glad* (rejoiced), *when they saw the Lord"* (John 20:20). Let us seek the Lord with all our hearts and then we will experience the joy of the Lord and that is a wonderful anticipation of the fullness of joy that will be our blessing in heaven.

> Joy is the serious business of heaven.
> *C. S. Lewis*

Perfect Peace

Peace is not the absence of trouble. Peace is the presence of God.

"The fruit of the Spirit is…peace" (Gal. 5:22, NIV). This quality of peace can seem utterly elusive to many people today. One pointed to some words on a display board at a Bible Exhibition and said, "That's what I need." The words said, "Peace of Heart". Another person asked me whether it was actually possible to ever know real peace of heart and mind. So many people in our contemporary society are in a desperate search for true peace. I believe we can not only find such peace but can experience it as a reality in our lives.

When we think of peace in our modern world there is a tendency to view it in a negative sense. As we talk of the political, military and international areas of life we define peace as the absence of strife. If we are not at war, then we are at peace. In the home we define peace as the absence of noise, argument or disturbance. Yet peace that is a fruit of the Spirit is much more positive. It is a wholeness, a community of people in a right relationship with each other and with God. It is a wholeness that pervades, affects and positively influences the situations and people with whom we find ourselves. This is encapsulated in the beautiful word with which Jewish people greet each other, "Shalom" and that carries the idea of completeness, rest, ease, security and unity.

When a group of hijackers commandeered a plane many years ago the passengers went through a horrific experience. Eventually the captives were released and the television cameras filmed them leaving the plane. One lady came down the steps and had clearly been through a frightening and terrible ordeal and yet in her arms was her baby. The baby was contentedly sleeping and the caption was "peace in turmoil". Clearly the baby was unaware of what was happening and could be perfectly peaceful in its mother's arms. Yet that can be our peace even in the midst of horrendous circumstances. Nothing need rob us of this glorious peace which is a fruit of the Spirit.

Yet so many people live with an absence of peace. A woman spoke with me after a church service some years ago and she was deeply afraid of death. Someone had told her that she had a short life line and she was deeply disturbed as a result. We needed to pray with her and bring to her heart the reassurance of the gospel. Another person told me of her fear for her children growing up in a turbulent world and she feared for them to the extent that she could not sleep. However, the Christian developing the fruit of the Spirit need not be troubled, anxious or worried either about the future or death. We know the Lord and He is able to remove all doubts and worries and also He knows the future and holds it in His hands.

For the Christian peace is not simply the absence of conflict or an artificial state induced by tranquillizers, but a deep and abiding calmness which only God can produce in our hearts and minds. Thus when we yield to worry, doubt and anxiety we are in reality sinning because we are denying the Lord the right to lead us in peace and confidence. So we grieve the Spirit when we yield to worry. It is very easy to take our eyes off the Lord and forget the greatness of God and so give way to worry. The best way to peace is prayer as a genuine reaching out for the presence of Almighty God in our lives.

The Bible reveals two kinds of peace.

1. PEACE WITH GOD

"Therefore, since we have been justified through faith, we have peace with God through our Lord Jesus Christ."   Romans 5:1, NIV

Before we can ever know the inner peace that is a fruit of the Spirit we must firstly know peace with God. This is the end of our enmity, rebellion and warfare with God demonstrated by our sinful words, deeds and thoughts. It is about reconciliation with God. This made possible by the death and resurrection of the Lord Jesus. Jesus secured the means of our reconciliation with God and all we have to do is accept it by receiving Christ into our lives through repentance and faith. This is made clear in the following verses make clear.

> *"…when we were God's enemies, we were reconciled to him through the death of his Son."*
> Romans 5:10, NIV

> *"For he himself is our peace, who has made the two one and has destroyed the barrier, the dividing wall of hostility…"* Ephesians 2:14, NIV

> *"And through him to reconcile to himself all things…by making peace through his blood, shed on the cross."* Colossians 1:20, NIV

This peace is a gift because it is not a human but a divine achievement. We are united with God through Christ and are no longer His enemies but His friends and can live in deep fellowship with Him.

2. PEACE OF GOD

To know the God of peace enables us to experience the peace of God in our hearts. This is clearly shown us in Philippians 4:7: *"And the peace of God, which passeth all understanding, shall keep your hearts and minds through Christ Jesus."*

This is a deep calm in our souls. The great Indian Christian, Sadhu Sundar Singh before he came to know Christ as Saviour was in a desperate search for truth. One day he was in deep despair and contemplated suicide. At that point he had a vision of Christ and a deep peace permeated his heart. The vision faded never to reappear but the peace remained forever.

This peace is found in the will of God as Isaiah wrote, *"You will keep in perfect peace him whose mind is steadfast, because he trusts in you. Trust in the Lord forever, for the Lord, the Lord, is the Rock eternal"* (Isa. 26:3-4, NIV). However we must never look at the fruit, our attention should always be on the source of that fruit, namely the Lord. Once we glory in the fruit we lose sight of the Giver. The great preacher C. H. Spurgeon once said, "I looked at Christ and the dove of peace flew into my heart. I looked at the dove of peace and it flew away!" To know more of the fruit of the Spirit and of this peace we must keep our eyes firmly fixed upon the Saviour. We must meditate upon Him and so be lifted above the circumstances and feelings that can get us down. We must keep close to Christ who is ultimately the source of our peace.

3. THE PEACE OF CHRIST

Certainly the Lord Jesus knew a wonderful peace with God His Father. There was an eternal oneness between the members of the Trinity. Indeed He could say, *"I am in the Father and the Father is in me"* (John 14:11, NIV). As a result he demonstrated the peace of God in His earthly life and was the most calm, restful and peaceful person that it was possible to know. The message He proclaimed was peace and a peace that reflected His character as Peter made clear in Acts 10:36, *"...telling the good news of peace through Jesus Christ, who is Lord of all"* (NIV). This was not a false peace engendered by moral compromise or surrender of principle. This was real and genuine and stemmed from deep communion with His Father. That is why He could speak of *"my peace"* (John 14:27, NIV).

If His peace had been based simply upon favourable circumstances or upon people who supported and sided with Him then He would have very soon lost it. This was because His popularity began to fade, His disciples fell away, hostility towards Him opened up and the shadows around Him deepened. In the end He suffered humiliation, abandonment, pain and martyrdom and yet His peace never left Him. This was because His peace had a spiritual source. Firstly He was obedient to God and that is the real secret of peace which permeates heart and mind. His will was fully surrendered to His Father's and there was no wickedness in Him. The prophet Isaiah wrote, *"If only you had paid attention to my commands, your peace would have been like a river…"* (Isa. 48:18, NIV). The Lord heeded the commands and knew deep and real peace. Secondly He also had a purpose and mission. Like a river His life flowed in one direction. He had one purpose and He would not be deflected from it but was totally loyal to it. He thus possessed peace and was able to impart peace. It may be that the restlessness found amongst many people today, especially young people, is due to a lack of purpose, direction or aim in life. Thirdly, the Saviour was always in communion with His Father as each day He engaged in prayer. Sometimes He spent all night in prayer, at other times He was up before dawn to pray. Communion with God leads to the peace of God in the heart. Finally we can say that the Saviour was anointed by the Spirit of God and lived under the Spirit's control. The fruit of the Spirit in a surrendered life is peace.

Thus to really know peace we also need to be obedient to the Lord and to know His purpose for our lives. It is a very great testimony when we maintain peace and contentment in our lives, even when things seem to be going badly for us.

HINDRANCES TO PEACE

There are a lot of enemies to inner peace and all of them ultimately derive from Satan and selfishness. The Devil does not want Christians to live in peacefulness and he has achieved his objective if he can disturb the peace of God's people, by making them restless and unstable.

SIN

The first and obvious enemy of peace is sin. The Old Testament says, *"But the wicked are like the tossing sea, which cannot rest, whose waves cast up mire and mud. 'There is no peace,' says my God, 'for the wicked'"* (Isa. 57:20-21, NIV). There can never be any coexistence between deliberate sin and the peace of God. When sin enters the life then peace disappears. If this happens then we need to confess our sin to the Lord in repentance and renounce it before Him. This may involve saying "sorry" to people we may have hurt and seeking the Saviour's help to guard against sin in the future.

WORRY

It is all too easy to succumb to worry and anxiety. People worry and can be disturbed over their looks, their school or college examinations, money and a host of other things. Unless this enemy is conquered we can never know a continuation of peace. In Matthew 6:25-34 the Lord Jesus emphasized the words *"do not worry"* (Matt. 6:25, NIV) and clearly was emphasizing to His disciples that they must conquer anxiety. Worry often stems from fear and we may remember the school bully who made us afraid and we lived with the worry that he might pick on us. The antidote was strong action and that allayed fear and dealt a deathblow to worry. Yet always the best antidote in terms of action is prayerfulness. There is nothing more important than talking to God about our troubles and problems. So if we are in danger of becoming worried then we should turn to God in prayer. True prayerfulness will bring a beautiful peace to our hearts and minds. This is what the apostle Paul meant when he wrote, *"Do not be anxious about anything, but in everything, by prayer and petition, with thanksgiving, present your requests to God. And the peace of God, which transcends all understanding, will guard your hearts and your minds in Christ Jesus"* (Phil. 4:6-7, NIV). Genuine prayer is the answer to worry. Being prayerful about everything means that we will be anxious about nothing.

AMBITION

This is the desire to be successful and get to the top of the corporate ladder and is a deep drive in human nature. It is sometimes described today as "the rat race" and one song writer penned the following words, "You're struggling and striving and doing the driving and look where its getting you—absolutely nowhere." The values of a modern material-istic society are the need to get on, to achieve and to possess and yet not all ambition is wrong. The sad part is that ambi-tion can be corrupted and tainted by selfishness and can all too easily make people twisted, bitter and churned up inside when an ambition is thwarted. Jeremiah the Old Testament prophet seems to have been aware of this danger when he wrote, *"Should you then seek great things for yourself? Seek them not"* (Jer. 45:5, NIV). The answer to ambition is contentment as one writer has said, "Complain of nothing; never compare your lot with that of another; never picture yourself to your-self in any circumstances in which you are not, never dwell on the morrow."

Certainly the apostle Paul had learned to be content as he wrote, *"I am not saying this because I am in need, for I have learned to be content whatever the circumstances. I know what it is to be in need, and I know what it is to have plenty. I have learned the secret of being content in any and every situation, whether well fed or hungry, whether living in plenty or in want. I can do every-thing through him who gives me strength"* (Phil. 4:11-13, NIV). Contentment goes hand in hand with peace and we should learn to be content in the Lord with our material possessions and our status.

OVER ACTIVITY

Over activity is often linked with driving ambition and is another serious threat to inner peace in modern society and especially for the Christian, who might have a high pres-sured job and then comes home to family and church respon-sibilities. The result is that time is short and it is all too easy to be rushed, overburdened, frantic, tense and tired. In the hectic pace to do what we think we should do we can lose the peace of God in our hearts. The antidote is to be selective and that requires very deep spiritual wisdom. Yet our greatest example is the Saviour as we never read of Him running because He was never in a rush and was never late! While here on earth He did not try to evangelize the whole earth but lived and worked with no frantic hassle. He confined Himself to the land of Israel and even there only healed a select few and seized just a few of the opportunities presented to Him for service. He was very selective and many times by-passed opportunities to do good work because it was a lesser priority. We would do well to follow the Saviour's example.

MOODS

These are emotional responses which can last for considerable periods of time and can consist of irritability, resentment or lust and all are hindrances to peace. Sometimes it is simply feeling low and if taken to extremes can be dangerous and lead to real despondency, discouragement, depression and despair. Our moods rise and fall according to our feelings and when we are in a bad mood others have to be very careful what they say to us and maybe will wait for us to be in a good mood to ask a question. It is important that we learn not to depend upon moods and not be driven by feelings. We must learn to depend upon the will and purpose of God for our lives. Peace and purpose go very much together. We should have a goal and persist in achieving that goal and battle towards its fulfilment no matter how we feel and no matter what obstacles might be in the way.

NEGATIVE THINKING

It is not only our emotions but also our thoughts that can be a hindrance to peace. It is possible to develop a habit of thinking negatively and to continually regret the past or think we are inferior to others. This can lead to a defeatist outlook and give real fear about the future. Such thinking can lead to serious loss of inner peace. The antidote is positive thinking. Robert F. Kennedy said, "Some men see things as they are and ask why? I see things which never were and ask, why not?" The Christian can certainly say that God is able to do what seems to us an impossibility and so we must capture a vision of the greatness of God. Also to think positively is to think in a Christian way and Paul mentions this by saying, *"Finally, brethren, whatsoever things are true, whatsoever things are honest, whatsoever things are just, whatsoever things are pure, whatsoever things are lovely, whatsoever things are of good report; if there be any virtue, and if there be any praise, think on these things"* (Phil. 4:8). So we need to keep our mind and thoughts upon the Word of God and upon our Saviour, the Lord Jesus Christ and the negative will go and the positive will come and with it the wonderful peace of God.

May we continually know the reality of the fruit of the Spirit which is peace in our hearts and lives.

> The Peace of God is that eternal calm which lies far too deep in the praying, trusting soul to be reached by any external disturbances.
>
> *A. T. Pierson*

Longsuffering or Patience

> Our patience will achieve more than our force.
>
> *Edmund Burke*

"The fruit of the Spirit is…patience" (Gal. 5:22, NIV). Every true Christian should be developing genuine patience in their character and for some this might be naturally easier than for others. Essentially this has to do with our relationships with other people and it is all too easy to be impatient and even irritable with what we perceive to be the awkwardness or indifference of others towards us. Yet how we react to other people reveals what sort of Christians we really are and the patient Christian has the ability to help, strengthen and encourage others in their faith.

This word *"patience"* is sometimes translated as *"long-suffering"* and obviously carries the idea of being able to suffer over a prolonged period of time without losing one's temper or composure. It is as one person has written, "steadfast-ness under provocation". This may be provocation simply for being a Christian and therefore for the early Christians who were hounded, imprisoned, beaten and persecuted this was a challenge to endure despite all that they suffered. The concept of patience thus involves enduring ill treatment and pressure without anger or any thought of retaliation and revenge and certainly entertaining no thought of giving up. It really is to suffer long.

TO BE LIKE JESUS

For many of us it may be all too easy to strike out with anger when we are provoked by work colleagues, neighbours, fellow church members, family members, school or college colleagues and yet to do so fails to show the fruit of the Spirit. To see true patience in action is a wonderful testimony of the power of Jesus Christ. One man saw how Christians reacted under pressure and said, "When I saw the unwearied patience…I became a Christian." George Dempster was a Christian minister in London and had a great ministry amongst the working classes. He dressed as a docker and queued for work in the early morning cold so that he could be alongside the men and lead them to Christ. One day his job was to load barges which entailed moving across a plank from one barge to another and a joke was played on him. The plank was "jiggled" and he fell into the mud below. The men laughed as he struggled through the mud and regained his footing, but as he climbed back to the quayside they drifted back to their work. One man remained and said that he had been impressed with the patient reaction of George Dempster and that became the prelude to the man's conversion to Christ. We must be very careful how we react to others.

THE PATIENCE OF JESUS

The Lord Jesus was the most patient of people. We see it in His teaching as He had to continually repeat His message because the disciples were so slow to learn and found it difficult to understand. It was certainly slow work teaching them. Yet what He taught was not intrinsically complicated but went very much against everything they had been taught and what they had accepted as normal. Indeed every teacher needs to be patient with inattentive pupils who may be slow to learn. So Jesus had to be patient with dull disciples, with fickle crowds who came to Him for the wrong reasons and who drifted away very quickly. He was patient with the sick and disabled and even with His enemies who tried to trap Him with trick questions.

However His patience was most fully tested when He endured the torture, trial, humiliation, mockery and unjust accusations after He was falsely arrested. Yet even as He was nailed to the cross He could say, *"Father, forgive them; for they know not what they do"* (Luke 23:34). Our Lord demonstrated the most wonderful patience and truly suffered long. There was no calling down the wrath or judgement of God upon His enemies. He lived in such harmony with the Holy Spirit that He was never irritable, resentful, vengeful or malicious, because such features are never the results of the work of the Holy Spirit.

Patience is a delightful petal of the flower of love. When we are motivated by love for people then we are willing to be patient with them and suffer their failings and even insults. Thus every Christian should be willing to show "patience in love" to all people without exception.

PERSEVERANCE

Patience also carries the idea of perseverance. It is to persevere or keep going under the most awful strain. It is to maintain our calling to serve Christ no matter what the persecution, provocation or even the terrible weariness that can be experienced in ministry. We remember that in the Old Testament the Israelite leader Gideon with a very small army of 300 men defeated the host of Midian and pursued the survivors. We read of Gideon and his men that they were *"faint, yet pursuing them"* (Judg. 8:4). They were weary to the point of exhaustion but they did not give up. In the New Testament we are instructed that *"having done all, to stand"* (Eph. 6:13), which means that even when we feel that we have done everything possible then we should still maintain our calling for God and never give up. Never, for one moment, should the idea of defeat or of throwing in the towel enter our minds.

Patience is a great and attractive quality that should be seen in the Christian life. Yet too often it can be weakened by selfishness, anger or ill will and then impatience and frustration can overtake us. We need to wake up and remember that the problem is not God but us. We need to renounce and confess our failings in repentance before God and seek His power to conquer them.

ANGER

Anger is not necessarily incompatible with patience though we would naturally think that to be angry negates the whole idea of patience. Yet as we read our Bible we find that God is an angry God, even though He is a God of wonderful patience (Ps. 86:15) because we read, *"In his anger against Israel"* (Judg. 2:14, NIV). So clearly in God there is compatibility between anger and patience. Also we read of the Lord Jesus, *"He looked around at them in anger"* (Mark 3:5, NIV) and again *"When Jesus saw this, he was indignant"* (or angry) Mark 10:14, NIV). So in the Lord Jesus we see both anger and patience and so the two are not contradictory or inconsistent with each other. Clearly there must be times when it is sinful to be angry and at other times it would be sinful not to be angry! The reason being that we must draw a distinction between what we could call "good anger" and "bad anger". The essential difference between these two kinds of anger are where the centre, focus and underlying cause lies.

GOOD OR RIGHTEOUS ANGER

This is anger that reacts to evil, injustice and brutality towards people other than ourselves. Such anger in the face of evil is good anger. Abraham Lincoln saw the evil of slavery and was deeply angered by the treatment of slaves in his country. His anger was expressed in the words, "If ever I get a chance to hit that thing, I'll hit it hard." Thus good anger is kindled by wrong done to others and is a real and genuine sign of concern for their welfare. Such anger is not self-motivated but motivated by a deep care and love for others. In the cases sighted of Jesus being angry it was anger directed towards those who tried to keep people away from the liberating message of the gospel and away from the love of the Father. God's anger was directed to those who worshipped inanimate objects and refused to seek the living God who could richly bless them.

BAD OR SELFISH ANGER

This is self-centred and is an outburst of irritability, bad temper or vindictiveness because of some perceived or real injustice done to me. There can be two problems with bad anger.

A. THE ANGRY OUTBURST: a politician from a former era was known for such angry outbursts that during them veins stood out on his forehead and his advisors talked of him having "veiners". If we are prone to such outbursts then we must always be ready to seek delay or a cooling off period. Someone has said, "When angry count to ten, when very angry count to a hundred" and that is sound advice. Never make decisions or send messages when in the middle of such an outburst. It will inevitably be regretted later. There is apparently a Chinese proverb that says, "If you are patient at one moment of anger, you will escape a hundred days of sorrow."

B. THE ANGRY MOOD: this is even more dangerous than the angry outburst. This lingers and is the harbouring of a grudge or a cherished resentment. Recently I heard of a couple who decided to leave their church. In their letter of resignation they cited an incident of twelve years before. No one could remember the incident but it had lingered as an angry, seething focus in their lives for all those years. However even good anger can be corrupted if it is allowed to settle upon a life. That is why the New Testament says, *"In your anger do not sin: Do not let the sun go down while you are still angry"* (Eph. 4:26, NIV). It is imperative that we learn to overcome both the angry outburst and the angry mood if we are to become effective in our Christian life and testimony.

We need to learn the exercise of patience in all areas of life and to show the restraint that comes along with such exercise. Patience needs to be shown to everyone and here we focus upon three areas of life: upward towards God, outward towards people and inward with ourselves.

1. PATIENCE WITH GOD

This is not meant to be blasphemous and may seem a strange thing to say but so often we earnestly pray and yet there seems to be no answer to our prayers. We appeal to God for help and no help appears to come. We may feel like the psalmist who wrote, *"Awake, O Lord! Why do you sleep? Rouse yourself! Do not reject us for ever"* (Ps. 44:23, NIV). The psalmist knew that God did not sleep and also that God does not forget His people. Yet he seems to be impatient with God, even irritable that there is no answer to his prayer.

Our impatience with God is bound up with our misunderstanding of time because God's time is often not the same as ours and we must realize that God's timing is always the best for us. God may appear to be slow but we need to learn to wait for the Lord's answers knowing that the true blessing will arrive at the right time. In the mean time we must keep praying to the Lord, even though it has been years and may yet be more years before He answers us.

The Lord sometimes delays His answers to test our resolve. Do we mean what we pray or do we give up and stop our prayers? Also through it all we are called to trust the Lord and wait to hear His voice, as the prophet Habakkuk wrote: *"If it seems slow, wait for it; it will surely come; it will not delay"* (Hab. 2:3, ESV). Let us keep praying and with patience anticipate the answer from the Lord. The poet put it this way: "His wisdom is sublime, His heart profoundly kind, God never is before His time, And never is behind." Philip Brooks (the famous Boston Pastor) was once asked the reason for his agitation and replied, "The trouble is I am in a hurry, but God isn't!" James Packer wrote, "Patience means living out the belief that God orders everything for the spiritual good of His children."

2. PATIENCE WITH PEOPLE

The Bible says that *"love is patient"* (1 Cor. 13:4, NIV) and so to be patient with others is to demonstrate a loving response to them. Also we read, *"be patient with everyone"* (1 Thess. 5:14, NIV). That is very easy to obey when life is going smoothly and people are easy going but it is a different story when things get difficult. Let us consider three such difficulties.

A. **UNTIMELY INTERRUPTIONS:** such interruptions can stop us doing important work and also disrupt our leisure time or sleep patterns. In such circumstances it may be easy to react with anger, resentment and tell others to be more courteous and we may even feel that we have the right to be angry. Yet as we remember the Saviour He was in desperate need of rest and yet the crowds came and His reaction was not resentment but compassion. We need to be totally available for people and be ready to help them in their need no matter when that need arises. How we react to untimely interruptions is a good indication of how patient we are. On some occasions people have telephoned in the middle of the night and made a request for help. It may be easy to feel irritated or angry but their need does not wait for convenient hours and so the call of the Lord is to see interruptions as opportunities to serve the Lord by meeting the needs of people.

B. **NEGATIVE CRITICISM:** it is interesting to see how we react when attention is drawn to our imperfections, faults and failures. It is certainly easy to be resentful and to try justifying ourselves. Our instinctive reaction may be to criticize the critic more trenchantly than they have criticized us and yet a hasty answer may only make matters worse. We need to think about what is said. If it is true then we can take on board the criticism and we profit from what is told us. If it is untrue we can ignore those words and yet we have still profited by reacting in a Christlike manner. Someone has said, "We should accept criticism with creative patience. If it is true we are blessed, if it is untrue we are blessed."

C. HARSH WORDS: such words can wound very deeply especially if our motives have been mis-judged. Anger can easily be kindled and under the pressure of anger a response of harsh words may be engendered. It requires great calmness and patience to respond to harsh words with quietness. Yet Proverbs 15:1 says, *"A gentle answer turns away wrath, but a harsh word stirs up anger"* (NIV). Gracious words are powerfully effective, tempers cool, wrath is turned away and dissension is avoided. The Lord grant us such patience.

3. PATIENCE WITH OURSELVES

We must accept ourselves as we are and yet we must not stay as we are because there should be development and progress in our Christian lives and character. Yet such progress in not created and shaped by the Holy Spirit in a hurry and that is why we have the picture of fruit. Fruit is not developed overnight but is the result of a long process and so it is within our lives as the fruit of the Spirit is developed and seen in us. It is said that someone planted a bamboo seed in the ground and after one year there was nothing to be seen and it was the same each year for four years. It appeared that there was no growth. Then in the fifth year it grew to ninety foot. There had been small, even imperceptible growth in the earlier years and that would be the same for us.

TRIALS DEVELOP PATIENCE

Part of God's way in making us more patient is to allow trials and difficulties to come into our lives. It is through such experiences that the fruit of patience can be seen in us. This is made clear by the apostle James who wrote, *"count it all joy when ye fall into divers temptations; Knowing this, that the trying of your faith worketh patience"* (Jas. 1:2-3). Again we read, *"not only so, but we glory in tribulations also: knowing that tribulation worketh patience; And patience, experience; and experience, hope"* (Rom. 5:3-4).

So if we face trials and difficulties with the same attitude as Christ and in the power of His Spirit the end result will be patience. Thus we learn patience through the tribulations of life. Therefore they are to be welcomed as good for us and should never engender bitterness and anger. Let us first of all learn to be patient in the small things of life and in the inconsequential factors such as the queue jumper, the person who might jog us and so on. The true answer for patience is prayer. Yet some of our biggest problems are in the area of "Why?" and have to do with the issue of fairness. We must remember that we never see the full picture while here on earth and we must learn to trust the Lord and wait for Him to reveal all things. As we learn to be patient the Holy Spirit can use us and bless others but we too are richly blessed in the process.

Finally we must remember that patience is not an excuse for inaction. Jesus was not afraid to confront those who abused the temple in Jerusalem and turned the house of prayer into a den of thieves. We must not use patience as a reason for failing to do what is good and right and from confronting those who need to hear God's message. The saintly George Matheson once said, "There are times when I do well to be angry, but I have mistaken the times". Let us learn to be patient and exercise it for the glory of the Lord.

> To lengthen my patience is the best way to shorten my troubles.
> *George Swinnock*

The Kindness of Gentleness

We need power for gentleness.

Graham Scroggie

"The fruit of the Spirit is…gentleness" (Gal. 5:23, NIV), every Christian should develop this characteristic of gentleness in their everyday lives. Sometimes this word is translated as *"gentleness"* and carries the idea of "a kindness which pervades the whole of nature. A gentleness which washes away all that is hard and austere". Such gentleness is found in the Trinity as we read of *"thy gentleness"* (Ps. 18:35), the *"gentleness of Christ"* (2 Cor. 10:1) and gentleness as a fruit of the Holy Spirit. So true spiritual gentleness flows from the person of God and is found in a Christian's life through the work of the Holy Spirit.

Generally gentle kindness is a highly prized quality in our society and is seen by many people as a vital and essential requirement of human life. Indeed the general expectation is that Christians will be kind and often the two words "Christian" and "kindness" go together. So people might use the words, "She is a real Christian" and they are not talking about the lady's beliefs but about her kind and gentle nature and so because she is so kind then she is perceived as a Christian. Yet we must say that there are many people who are not Christians and who also show genuine kindness to others and tragically there are those who claim to be Christian and never reveal kindliness in their nature or in their dealings with other people. In such people the fruit of the Spirit is missing and it might be argued that they are not truly Christian. They are certainly not living lives that please God or benefit people.

Kindness is love in action and is summarized as follows.

> The best portion of a good man's life,
> His little, nameless, unremembered acts
> of kindness and of love.   *Wordsworth*

> Life is mostly froth and bubble,
> Two things stand alone,
> Kindness in another's trouble
> courage in your own.   *Adam Gordon*

Everywhere there are those who are lonely, housebound, disabled, depressed, bereaved, suicidal, redundant, unemployed, poor, divorced, ill, victims of accidents, tired, stressed, hurt, broken-hearted and yet they may look fine on the outside. Inside they may be full of pain with broken spirits and feelings of emptiness. Let us be people who do ROAK —Random Acts of Kindness. The world would be a much better place if there was an outbreak of kindness on a daily basis.

ACTS OF GENTLE KINDNESS

For many people life seems so superficial and transient and to be shown real and genuine kindness has an everlasting quality to it. I remember a lady in our street when we lived in a city in the Midlands of England. She was a widow living alone and had to be confined to a wheelchair as both legs had been amputated. She was very lonely and would sometimes sit at the doorway and watch the world go by. People passed her as they walked along but many ignored her and looked the other way. An act of kindness with a simple "Hello" would have made such a difference to her and we tried to help her and show her kindness as much as we could.

The story is told of the Russian author Y. Yevtushenko who at fifteen was on a geological expedition in Siberia and was so badly treated that he ran away. Eventually he fell into a ditch utterly exhausted. He was discovered by a peasant woman who came into the ditch and he said, "She pulled my hands away from my face. Intensely blue eyes between long black lashes looked at me with a warm kindness which is much better than pity". She took him home gave him food, a bath, a bed and deloused his clothes. He said, "I shall never forget her. Ever since then I have known that if all the values in this world are more or less questionable, the most important thing in life is kindness". Her reaction reminds us of the words of the Lord Jesus, *"For I was hungry and you gave me something to eat, I was thirsty and you gave me something to drink, I was a stranger and you invited me in, I needed clothes and you clothed me, I was sick and you looked after me, I was in prison and you came to visit me"* (Matt. 25:35-36, NIV).

The sign that we really belong to Christ and are truly developing the fruit of the Spirit is seen in the kindness we show. Acts of kindness are of great importance both in the eyes of the Saviour and as evidence of a genuine relationship with Him. Gentle kindness is bound up with the idea of graciousness and is reflected in thoughtfulness and courteousness. It is often seen in the small and seemingly insignificant areas of life. This was what Jesus meant when He said, *"And if anyone gives even a cup of cold water to one of these little ones because he is my disciple, I tell you the truth, he will certainly not lose his reward"* (Matt. 10:42, NIV). We may well be surprised at the significance of a word of encouragement, a phone call to the bereaved, a visit to the sick or a helping hand to those in need. We must be prepared to show kindness in the small activities of life and perhaps occasionally the need to show great kindness may be required of us.

Years ago I was with a colleague distributing gospel leaflets in the South Wales Valleys. It was a very hot day and we had no money to buy a drink and we sat down in the shade of a terraced house. A man came to his front door and took one look at us and went back inside. He returned with some water for us to drink. We expressed our thanks and were revived to continue the work and were blessed with a cup of cold water from a perfect stranger.

We remember that Mary of Bethany performed a great act of kindness upon the Lord when she poured her expensive perfume upon His feet. That perfume was very rare and would have cost a year's wages and was usually saved for a special occasion. Mary gave it as an act of worship to the Lord, knowing that she would never have another opportunity, as He was about to die for her sins on the cross. She seized the moment for expressing her devotion to the Saviour. We should likewise take every chance to demonstrate kindness as we bear in mind the words of someone who said, "I expect to pass through this world but once, any good thing therefore that I can do, or any kindness that I can show to any fellow-creature, let me do it now; let me not defer or neglect it, for I shall not pass this way again." Those words remind us just how vital and important it is to show kindness and gentleness which is a fruit of the Spirit.

THE GENTLENESS OF THE SAVIOUR

The Lord Jesus was the greatest example of gentle kindness that ever walked the earth. It dominated His life and ministry as He dealt with everyone (except the self-righteous, hypocritical religious leaders) with gentleness, kindness and compassion. In no way could He be described as hard, harsh or austere. He exercised great sensitivity and gentle compassion to the sick, the deranged, the lonely and the bereaved. To those who had deep scars and wounds in their spirits he was gentle and tender. He instinctively knew that there were lives that had been broken and battered by the storms of life and so He showed them a welcoming kindness.

His gentle, kind manner was obviously recognized by the children. Boys and girls instinctively know whether people love them or not. They flocked to Jesus because He deeply cared for them. We see them coming to Him and He put His arms around them and blessed them. He had time for them, even though they may have interrupted His teaching ministry but His love for them revealed how important they were to Him.

The story is told of an evangelist who was having a press conference in a hotel in the capital city of a South American country. All the main media players were there from the newspapers, the radio and the television. Part way through the conference a child of about ten came up to the evangelist, the son of the caretaker of the hotel. The child did not want an autograph but wanted to receive the Lord. That evangelist reflecting the love of Christ, broke up the important press conference and spent an hour counselling that child to faith in Christ. Ultimately if we show the fruit of the Spirit that is gentleness it will enable us to have our priorities ordered correctly and other people are much more important than any personal publicity we might engender.

THE GENTLENESS OF THE CHURCH

Gentle kindness has been and should always be the hallmark of the church. In the first century the New Testament highlights concerns amongst Christians and attempts to alleviate suffering caused by famine. In a similar way down through the centuries Christians have tried to alleviate hunger, pain, ignorance and depravation. So the Christian church has been in the forefront of building hospitals, schools, clinics, and orphanages, giving relief aid and helping to bring about social reform. Certainly this was true in Britain before the government took responsibility for these matters and clearly it has been the case in many developing nations. Indeed it would be true to say that many leaders of those nations would not have received any education had it not been for Christian missionaries setting up schools and teaching them to read and write. Many such leaders have acknowledged that enormous debt.

Someone has written, "One of the most glorious features of early Christianity was that it introduced a new kindliness

61

into the world—kindliness to children, kindliness to the poor, the destitute, plague ridden, kindliness to women who were given their rightful place in society, kindliness to common slaves who were not treated as beings of inferior clay but as a brother man, kindliness to men of alien races who were deemed fellow-members of the family of God; kindliness that led in due course to the abolition of gladiatorial combats."

Kindness is remembered long after the words of the preacher have been forgotten. The story is told of a lady who was so distressed in her soul that she rather nervously entered a church. She was unfamiliar with proceedings and unsure where to sit down. One lady smiled at her brightly and welcomed her warmly and invited the lady to sit by her. She helped her with the hymnbook and with the Bible reading and at the end of the service the lady went to see the preacher for counsel. She said that she had been moved by God during the service and so the minister enquired what part of his message had got home to her. She had to admit that none of it had, as she had failed to understand what he had been talking about. So he asked what hymn or prayer or reading had touched her heart and again she disappointed him by saying she could not fathom the meaning of the hymns, could not follow the prayers and the reading was too deep for her. So he asked, "Well why have you come to see me?" She replied, "Because that lady was so kind and I felt the love of God as she gently helped me during the service." Kindness makes a very great impact and is certainly remembered for a long time. However we must also remember that an act of unkindness is also never forgotten and we must never be unkind. I have met too many people who claim that they want nothing to do with the church because a so-called Christian was unkind to them.

We need to show kindness and keep on showing kindness. If we have failed in the past then let us repent and seek God's help to show this fruit of the Spirit in our lives and in our everyday relationships. It can be too easy to be so tunnel-visioned about our activities and the organisations to which we belong that we can easily lose sight of the need to show kindness. Such an approach is fostered by the thought that the government or social services provide all that is needed for those who have problems. Also we have a disdain for sin, indeed a hatred of it and that is right because the Lord Himself hates sin. Yet in hating sin we should never be unkind, harsh or show hatred to the sinner. Like the Saviour we should love sinners, while at the same time hating their sin.

When I lived in the city of Coventry in the West Midlands our church was situated very near to the city centre. As a consequence we had many unusual people turning up at our door with all manner of bizarre requests. Many of them had addiction problems, others had prison records and some were tramps. They were people badly scarred by life, with deep wounds in their spirits and of course many of them simply wanted to gain some money to fuel their addiction problem. We learned to try and show them kindness, though we quickly learnt that to give money was never the answer. Some appreciated the help we gave to secure a train ticket or some food, while others were quite abusive when we refused to hand over cash. At times it was tough but like all Christians we were called to show genuine Christian kindness.

In showing kindness we might not always be thanked or appreciated. Yet that must never divert us because to show kindness is always the right thing to do. There must always be the balance between grace and truth. Truth is our religious code, the sum of what we believe. Grace is the outworking of that truth into the practical areas of life. This means that we are slow to condemn and quick to show kindness and yet too often we may have been accused as Christians of the exact opposite—that we have been quick to condemn and slow to show kindness. Yet to win people for Christ we must always be kind and that might mean having to put up with rudeness and arrogance, to patiently answer questions that people throw at Christianity and go to people at the most inconvenient hours. Yet that is our calling and that is what the Saviour would do if He were in our situation.

TO BE LIKE JESUS

The apostle Paul put it this way, *"And the Lord's servant must not quarrel; instead, he must be kind to everyone, able to teach, not resentful. Those who oppose him he must gently instruct, in the hope that God will grant them repentance leading them to a knowledge of the truth"* (2 Tim. 2:24-25, NIV). The apostle James underlines the point when he writes, *"But the wisdom that comes from heaven is first of all pure; then peace loving, considerate, submissive, full of mercy and good fruit, impartial and sincere"* (Jas. 3:17, NIV). The Christian is called to show kindness as a reflection of the loving compassion that the Holy Spirit is engendering in his heart as he submits the authority of Jesus Christ.

We need to remember that gentle kindness does not mean weakness. Abraham Lincoln was noted for his gentle humility but was not perceived as weak. He had great strength of character and it was that combination of strength and compassion that made him so great and he comes down through history as possibly the greatest president of the United States. Thus, as someone has written, "The gentle heart is the broken heart and is the heart that weeps over the sins of the bad, as well as the sacrifices of the good."

Kindness can really be used by God to transform lives and we see an example of this in the New Testament in the case of Zacchaeus (Luke 19). There was a man who was a political collaborator and a morally corrupt person. He was despised by the Israelite population and was considered utterly reprehensible and respectable people were scandalized when Jesus went to his house for a meal. Yet that act of kindness deeply impressed Zacchaeus and he was transformed from a grasping tax collector who lined his own pockets to a paragon of generosity. Half of all he possessed he gave to the poor and the other half was used to make restitution of all that he had unfairly taken in the past. Thus he was converted by kindness and was wonderfully converted to kindness.

It has been rightly said, "Genuine conversion always leads to the display of a kindlier spirit towards others." Kindness is a language that is understood everywhere and it can be seen by the blind and heard by the deaf. It is said that when Christian missionaries went to a certain part of Papua New Guinea that to begin with the natives did not understand their theology but they understood their loving kindness and allowed themselves to be won by it. That is a glorious wonder and so we should all show the fruit of the Spirit that is gentle kindness or as the Apostle Paul wrote: *"Be kind to one another, tenderhearted, forgiving one another, as God in Christ forgave you"* (Eph. 4:32, ESV).

> Gentle words fall lightly, but they have great weight.   *Derek Bingham*

Generous Goodness

No man knows how bad he is until he has tried
to be good.   *C. S. Lewis*

"The fruit of the Spirit is...goodness" (Gal. 5:22, NIV). It is important that every Christian develops the fruit of goodness and yet in our modern society the word "good" has been corrupted. It had been devalued to the level of the "do gooder". This is the sort of person who may be upright but is utterly unattractive and who may come across as superior and someone who knows what is best for us. Such people can be extremely irritating and it might be possible to respect their dignity, knowledge and discipline, but we would not want them as friends.

Yet goodness as a fruit of the Spirit is a highly attractive quality. It is essentially about making good more attractive than evil. The Lord Jesus triumphed over evil not by excluding it, in the sense of see no evil and hear no evil, but by making goodness more attractive. It is said that the great Christian St. Augustine had been a slave to sexual lust before he was converted to Christ. Even as a Christian he could not break the habit of lust but it was overcome in his life by the Lord and replaced with sovereign joy, which was something far sweeter than all sexual pleasure. He was released by the wonder of the presence of Christ.

Naturally speaking none of us has any goodness that would make us acceptable to God. Indeed the New Testament says, *"there is no one who does good, not even one"* (Rom. 3:12, NIV). We possess no inherent goodness, no spiritual goodness, yet in Christ we can know and experience the quality of goodness which is produced by the power of His Holy Spirit. Such goodness was most perfectly seen in the person of the Lord Jesus. In Christ there was complete sinlessness in His character and He had an absence of any flaw or defect. Yet His goodness was also a vital, positive and highly attractive quality because it drew great crowds who loved to see Him, talk with Him and listen to what He said. Such goodness can be ours as we look at, listen to and obediently follow the Saviour. We need to consider two aspects of goodness.

1. BEING GOOD

This is essentially what we are and has to do with character. The great Greek philosopher Aristotle once said, "Make a habit of doing good and you will become good. Speak and do virtuous things and you will become virtuous". Such words are not strictly true but they carry an element of truth. Certainly good people do become better by habit but evil people do not. It is the motive of the heart that is all-important. A hypocrite can put on an act by saying and doing right things and it may not be easily discerned. Yet in the end the hidden is revealed and the essential character comes to light, for a tree is known by its fruit. The Lord Jesus says, *"There is nothing concealed that will not be disclosed, or hidden that will not be made known"* (Luke 12:2, NIV).

So good character is a matter of the heart and it is essentially a heart that is right before God and from which flow good words and deeds. It is like a good spring from which flows good, clean water, so the good heart produces goodness. Indeed the heart is described as *"the wellspring of life"* (Prov. 4:23, NIV). To keep our hearts clean we need to know Jesus as our Saviour and each day keep close to Him through prayer, renewal and obedience. Thus goodness is about being good within, having a clean and pure heart. This means that we then do the right thing for the right motive.

2. DOING GOOD

This is not so much about character as conduct. We read of the Saviour, *"how he went around doing good"* (Acts 10:38, NIV). So we witness an innate goodness in the Lord, His character was one of unalloyed goodness and that was clearly seen in His conduct. Someone once wrote. "I read in a book, that a man called Christ went about doing good. It is very disconcerting to me that I am so easily satisfied with just—going about!" We must be careful that what we do is of worth in the eyes of the Lord because it is His will and not just doing what our own inclinations encourage us to do.

So Jesus emphasized goodness of heart not because He devalued good deeds but because He was deeply concerned about conduct. He was well aware that only out of a good heart and inner motive can truly flow good deeds and conduct. Thus He says, *"By their fruit you will recognize them… every good tree bears good fruit, but a bad tree bears bad fruit"* (Matt. 7:16-17, NIV). Again He says, *"The good man brings good things out of the good stored up in him, and the evil man brings evil things out of the evil stored up in him"* (Matt. 12:35, NIV). So character and conduct are so deeply bound up as to be virtually inseparable and from a good heart good deeds flow spontaneously.

THE GOODNESS OF JESUS

Jesus constantly did what was good and His actions and words were a powerful blessing to everyone with whom He came in contact. He was always ready to preach the gospel and teach the Word of God. He was willing to feed the hungry, heal the sick, help the needy, find and save the lost. He truly gave Himself in service for the benefit of others. Many could say of the Saviour and of those who have followed in His footsteps, *"For I was hungry and you gave me something to eat, I was thirsty and you gave me something to drink, I was a stranger and you invited me in, I needed clothes and you clothed me, I was sick and you looked after me, I was in prison and you came to visit me"* (Matt. 25:35-36, NIV). Thus the idea of "goodness" is of being useful to other people. It is kindness in action and so takes very practical form. The New Testament knows nothing of inactive or impractical kindness! Essentially the idea of goodness is seen in terms of those who bestow benefits and thus we can think in terms of the words that begin with "bene" such as benevolent, benefactor, benefits.

The word carries the idea of generosity and usefulness and we see this very clearly in the case of a New Testament church leader, Barnabas.

THE EXAMPLE OF BARNABAS

In Acts 11:24 (NIV), we read that Barnabas was *"a good man"* and that he was *"full of the Holy Spirit"*. Those two aspects are closely related in that because he was filled with the Spirit of God, then he demonstrated that wonderful quality of goodness and was generous in very large measure. We see that he was generous in three important areas of life.

A. HIS MATERIAL POSSESSIONS (ACTS 4:26)

Barnabas was of Jewish descent that belonged to the Jewish tribe of Levi. He came to Jerusalem from Cyprus where he owned some land. He sold that land and gave all the proceeds to the Lord. He held nothing back and that was in stark contrast with a couple called Ananias and his wife Sapphira. They sold some property and pretended to give all the proceeds to the Lord, but their hypocrisy was exposed and they were judged by the Lord (Acts 5:1-11). Barnabas was originally known as Joses but was given the name Barnabas by the apostles. Barnabas means "son of consolation or encouragement" and certainly Barnabas gave great encouragement to fellow Christians by not being materialistically minded. Here was a generous man which reflected his heart of goodness.

B. HIS REACTION TO PEOPLE (ACTS 9:27)

The generosity of Barnabas extended further than simply his attitude to material possessions. He was also generous towards people. When the recently converted **Saul of Tarsus** went back to Jerusalem and wanted to join the Christians they refused him. They could not believe that this persecutor was truly a disciple of the Lord and they were afraid to allow him entry in case it was all an elaborate trick to trap the Christians and cause them further and more intensive persecution. However, Barnabas took Saul and introduced him to the apostles and assured them that Saul was truly converted to Christ. Thus on the word of Barnabas, Saul was accepted by the church of God. We realize that Barnabas was taking a risk because if Saul was subsequently found to be false who would ever have believed Barnabas again? So at the risk of his own credibility he befriended Saul and recommended him to the church. One wonders what would have happened if Barnabas had not been there? Maybe Saul would have been so discouraged that he might have given up and never become the great apostle and missionary of later years. Maybe he would never have written the bulk of the New Testament. However, we thank God that Barnabas was there and Saul was received into the body of the church.

When Paul and Barnabas were about to set out on the second missionary journey **John Mark** wanted to join them. He had deserted the missionaries on the first journey and so had come home in some disgrace. Indeed Paul was so unsure whether he was restored to fellowship with the Lord that he refused to take him, while Barnabas was convinced and took him on missionary work to Cyprus. Again if Barnabas had not been so generous would Mark have been so discouraged that he never wanted to serve the Lord again and we would have been denied the second book of the New Testament, the gospel of Mark. Again we thank God that Barnabas did encourage Mark and drew him back into Christian service. Barnabas was certainly generous towards people.

C. HIS ATTITUDE TO THE WORK OF GOD (ACTS 11:22-25)

The church at Antioch unlike the church at Jerusalem was of mixed nationality. There were both Jews and Gentile and as a result there were certain tensions and so the apostles decided to send someone they could trust to oversee the work in Antioch. The person they sent was Barnabas and after he had been there a while and assessed the situation he realized that he needed someone who was more gifted than himself to do the work properly. He needed someone well-versed in the Old Testament and who was a convincing speaker and so he went looking for that right person and brought Saul of Tarsus to Antioch. The result was that Saul took the public role and increasingly became the leader while Barnabas took a much more secondary role. This did not seem to cause any problems for Barnabas and he did not complain that his position, which had been appointed by the apostles, was being superseded. A less generous person might have been resentful but not Barnabas because the work of God was more important to him than his own personal standing. Barnabas was generous in the work of God.

It is very evident that Barnabas was one of the most attractive characters in the New Testament and as a result of his goodness reflected in his generosity many people were added to the church in Antioch. So his goodness was seen in generosity of his hand, he gave; the generosity of his mind, he accepted others and the generosity of his heart, he shared and loved. When goodness is seen in this light it is a highly attractive and desirable quality.

THE DEVELOPMENT OF GOODNESS

As Christians we need to see the development of this wonderful quality in our lives because so often any goodness in us seems transient and shallow. It could be described as *"like the morning mist, like the early dew that disappears"* (Hos. 6:4). Ultimately this is the work of the Holy Spirit but we need to play our part.

ATTENTION

It is important and extremely helpful in the development of goodness to pay attention to the things of God. We need to divert attention away from ourselves and keep it upon Christ. This is very much a conscious effort at first but gradually we will find ourselves automatically focusing our mind upon the Lord and we will become like the object that we constantly focus upon. Thus we shall become like the Lord and will develop this fruit of goodness. Someone has said, "We shall advance more by contemplating Christ than by keeping our eyes fixed upon ourselves."

DEVOTION

The main ways in which we can keep our attention upon the Lord is to be devoted to the habits of prayer, fellowship and Bible study. We need to spend good quality time in study and meditation upon the Word of God and also in prayer and be devoted to attending meetings where others help us to focus upon the Lord. So we should be committed members of our local church and help in its activities.

RESTRAINT

While here on earth we will never be entirely Christ-like, that will happen in a future age when we are in heaven. At the moment there is an overlap between our old, self-centred nature which is sometimes called the "flesh" and our new nature in Christ known as the "spirit". There is conflict and tension between these two natures and that is a daily battle for every Christian believer. We do feel upset and disappointed when we fail the Saviour as the old nature reasserts itself and we wonder what progress we have made as Christians. Thus is it important to check, restrain, refuse and deny our old nature. This means we are careful where we go, what books we read, what films we watch and who we mix with, because so often these can trigger negative reactions that reveal something other than the quality of goodness. It may be hard and painful to exercise such restraint but it is essential for Christian growth and certainly the Christian life is one of personal discipline.

PRACTICE

The Christian characteristics or virtues that constitute the fruit of the Spirit will become established in our lives as we practice them. We must take every opportunity to practice this fruit of the Spirit that is goodness. This involves being good and doing good to those who may be our enemies or people with whom we don't really get along. We must never by-pass an opportunity of doing good and when we regularly practising this great quality it will become part and parcel of our character and of our every day lives. It would be a wonderful joy to think that it could be said of us in the words of the apostle Paul, *"I myself am convinced, my brothers, that you yourselves are full of goodness..."* (Rom. 15:14, NIV).

FINAL WARNING

We must never think that trying to be good and doing good will get us to heaven. Jesus is the only one who can enable us to reach the glory of the heavenly home. We need Him in our lives. This goodness which is a fruit of the Spirit is developed in those who know Jesus as Saviour and is a sign that they are already going to heaven. Such goodness glorifies God and pleases Him and is a very rich blessing to other people. May God enable us to develop this wonderful fruit.

A good life fears not life nor death.

Thomas Fuller

7

Faithful In All Things

I am not called to be successful, but faithful.

Mother Teresa

"The fruit of the Spirit is...faithfulness" (Gal. 5:22, NIV). We should as Christians be faithful. This word is sometimes translated as "faith" but is not the faith we exercise in Christ to become Christians, but the devotion to the Lord and His will which we exercise as Christians. The same word is translated as *"fidelity"* (NEB[7]) and it is about being loyal, reliable and firm. In the Roman world of the first century this was how a slave was expected to behave in total loyalty and faithfulness to his master. In a similar way husbands and wives are supposed to be faithful to each other and never be disloyal or unfaithful. Also in terms of membership of a local church, each individual member should be utterly faithful to that church and its aims and do all in their power to bring about the fulfilment of those aims.

Once again this is a highly attractive and desirable quality and we love to see it in our friends and family, especially in their relationship to ourselves. The apostle Paul wrote, *"...to show that they can be fully trusted, so that in every way they will make the teaching about God our Savior attractive"* (Titus 2:10, NIV). The Old Testament reminds us that loyalty to the Lord is very important. Israel had to wander in the desert for forty long and weary years because they proved to be disloyal and unfaithful to their God. May we be faithful and so never have that dreadful wilderness experience.

---

7   New English Bible (Oxford University Press and Cambridge University Press, 1961)

THE FAITHFULNESS OF CHRIST

The Lord Jesus was completely loyal to the will and purpose of His Father. Even as a boy of twelve when in the temple at Jerusalem He was totally aware of His responsibilities to carry out His Father's work and that was always the dominant desire of His heart. He said, *"My food…is to do the will of him who sent me and to finish his work"* (John 4:34, NIV). His food or the nourishment that sustained and strengthened Him was doing the will of God. Even when opposition to Him increased in Judaea and Jerusalem and friends urged Him to stay away He *"resolutely set out for Jerusalem"* (Luke 9:51, NIV). Nothing and nobody was able to divert Him from the call of God which He had to fulfil in Jerusalem.

Even in the agony of suffering endured in the Garden of Gethsemane, when the awfulness of what He was about to experience on the cross seemed to almost crush Him He was still not diverted from the Father's will. His prayer was simply, *"…not my will, but yours be done"* (Luke 22:42, NIV). Eventually He went to the cross and suffered and died for our sins. He was faithful even unto death and so it is no wonder that time and again in the last book of the Bible He is called "Faithful". He revealed that God's way of overcoming evil was by way of the cross and in approval of that great work God raised Him to life on the third day and has exalted Him to the highest place in heaven.

Jesus proved His faithfulness on earth and is now our faithful High Priest in heaven (Heb. 2:17) and one day He will come in power and will be revealed to all as the one who is *"called Faithful and True"* (Rev. 19:11, NIV). So He is not only faithful by nature but also faithful by name. It is always good for us as Christians to remember this characteristic of our Saviour and to walk in His footsteps as faithful Christians.

Sadly faithfulness is not a dominant characteristic of our modern society and this lack of loyalty has ruined many lives and shattered numerous families. It is a modern failing and in contrast the Christian church should be the place where the value of loyalty and faithfulness, both towards God and towards people, is reasserted, taught and practiced. It was so satisfying to read of a sincere Christian who had served the Lord over many years being described in the following terms after his death. "His Christian life was marked with consistency and dependability…Jim truly was a faithful brother."[8]

It has been a privilege to visit the wonderful Yellowstone National Park in the USA. It is famous for its geysers, which periodically shoot great spouts of water into the air. They are spectacular and the most famous and most popular is not the one where the water reaches the greatest height nor that lasts longest but is the one that is so regular and dependable that its actions can be timed. We were so fortunate to arrive just five minutes before it erupted and it is called "Old Faithful" because it is so dependable and regular. That is essentially what faithfulness is all about, being regular and dependable.

THE FAITHFULNESS OF CHRISTIANS

Such faithfulness can be seen in two ways. Firstly there is inner faithfulness where the Christian exercises devotion to contemplation, prayer and worship. The second is outer faithfulness where the Christian exercises devotion in action, practical matters and service. In Luke 10:38-42 there were two sisters Mary and Martha who exemplified these two aspects of faithfulness. Mary sat at the feet of Jesus and listened intently to His words. She sat in contemplation and worship of the Saviour. However Martha was preoccupied with work in the kitchen and there she served the Lord with active busyness.

INNER FAITHFULNESS

Here we follow the example of Mary and it is essentially our personal devotion to the Lord, which is enhanced,

---

8   Compiled by Robert Plant, *They Finished Their Course — Volume 4*, (Kilmarnock: John Ritchie, 2010), 50-51

strengthened and seen in three ways. Faithfulness in these three areas of our lives means regularity.

A. **PRAYER:** Prayer is stressed in Scripture, as a vital need for the Christian. In our personal lives prayer should be constant, regular and habitual. The Saviour told His disciples a parable *"to show them that they should always pray and not give up"* (Luke 18:1, NIV). Again the apostle Paul urged the Thessalonian Christians to *"pray continually"* (1 Thess. 5:17, NIV). In many ways this is extremely hard but Christians need to set rules and be determined to live by those rules. It is recognizing the problem that it is too easy to be governed by feelings and if we allow our feelings to dominate then our inconsistent natures will make us faithless instead of faithful in prayer. So we must be determined to consistently set aside a particular time each day to spend in prayer and nothing and nobody should interfere with that precious and essential time with the Lord. Also we should make every effort to be part of our church prayer meeting and never miss as it is the most vital meeting, often known as "the power house of the church".

B. **BIBLE STUDY:** we should develop the habit of constantly and intensively reading the Bible. This is God's revelation to mankind and we need to be devoted to reading its pages. We should not be put off from reading it by its length or the seeming difficulty of trying to understand it. We need to prayerfully engage in reading the Bible to hear the voice of God. It is important to read a short passage of the Bible at least once each day and meditate upon those words throughout the day. It is also good to read through the Bible in a year and gain an over or landscape view of the Holy Scriptures. There is also rich blessing in memorizing verses and passages of Scripture and in spending time in detailed study of the Word of God. All these things take time but if we are faithful in these areas of life we will find that our Christian life will make progress and blossom.

C. **CHURCH ATTENDANCE:** our personal devotion is greatly helped when we meet with fellow Christian believers. There we hear God's Word being read and expounded, we worship God and praise Him together and we can mutually encourage each other. It is all too often true that the isolated Christian who refuses to be committed in loyalty to his local church becomes the cold Christian and his devotion to the Lord becomes weak and is not characterized by faithfulness.

In our busy and hectic lives where we are called upon to be responsible for a seemingly endless list of activities we can never **find** the time for these things. So we must **make** the time and find the energy to fulfil our personal acts of devotion to the Lord in prayer, Bible study and church attendance. This may mean giving up things like watching so much television or going out with friends. This is not easy but we need disciplined and determined habits to be steadfastly sitting at the feet of Jesus. Yet it is there that we learn to be like Him in true faithfulness to the will and purpose of God for our lives. So we praise God for Mary and trust that we will be like her in personal devotion to the Lord.

OUTER FAITHFULNESS

Here we follow the example of Martha and there have been many who have denigrated the work of this New Testament lady. However the Saviour did not criticize her work or despise her contribution. Certainly communion with God is most important but service for God is also an essential and vital part of the Christian life. Indeed the two go very much together. Our inner devotedness should be seen in our outer devotedness. The one stems from the other and was clearly seen in the Lord Jesus. He was a man of prayer and a man of action. So Mary and Martha are linked together in revealing faithfulness to the Lord.

One sure test of faithfulness is in the small things of life and this was exactly what Jesus pointed out in the parable of the talents. He concluded the parable by saying, *"You have been faithful with a few things; I will put you in charge of many things"* (Matt. 25:21, NIV). It is important to be faithful in the small things of life such as not telling a white lie, not giving a false impression, not laughing at a dirty joke and not lifting inconsequential items in theft. If we take care to be faithful in such small matters then we are more likely to be faithful in the big things of life. Thus faithfulness is seen in how we discharge our responsibilities. We can look at four areas of our lives as Christians where we have responsibility and therefore should be faithful.

A. IN OUR GIVING: whether we worked for it, inherited it or were given it God entrusts money to us. We have a solemn responsibility and a sacred trust from God as to how we utilize our money. The widow in the New Testament gave two small coins to God's treasury and it was so insignificant in monetary value but it was all she had. She could give no more because she had donated one hundred percent of all she had. The principle given in the New Testament is set out in 1 Corinthians 16:2, *"On the first day of every week, each one of you should set aside a sum of money in keeping with his income"* (NIV). The idea is that giving should be regularly undertaken and needs to be thought about, with a particular amount set aside for the Lord's work. We should never just fish around at the last moment seeking some loose change to put into the collection. In the Old Testament they gave a tithe or a tenth and surely in the New Testament in the light of all that Jesus did for us on Calvary we should not give anything less! Also the amount is determined by income. The more we earn the more we should give and that is an obvious principle. Essentially giving is a reflection of our gratitude to God for the wonderful gift of His Son who came to earth and died to be our Saviour.

B. IN OUR WORK: we must remember that there are not two types of work, secular and sacred but that all work for the Christian should be considered the Lord's work. A friend of mine, who is a Christian, once applied for a job and was offered the job at the interview and the man who employed him said, 'I am taking you on because you don't simply work for me, but you work for God'. He recognized that Christians always serve a higher Master. Thus all work is covered with a very great dignity when we realize that ultimately we do it for the Lord. This will include paid work, namely our daily occupation and unpaid work, namely the voluntary and church work in which we engage. In all these areas we should be conscientious, honest, hard working and regular. This is not exactly spectacular or exciting and can at times be monotonous, boring and routine, especially if our work is repetitive. Yet we are called by the Lord to faithfully fulfil our tasks and do all out of loyalty to Christ.

C. IN OUR RELATIONSHIPS: when we interact with our friends and family members there should be very real trust. We should not knowingly let them down or break our promises to them. Indeed for friendship to be made and for friendship to flourish then faithfulness is of prime importance. This is love that is available at all times and reminds us that true friendship is all about loyalty. A loyal friend is always a source of unfailing strength and security. They can be relied upon even in the difficult circumstances of life. Yet the 'queen of friendships' is the intimacy of marriage, where one man and one woman are committed to each other for life. If that marriage relationship is to survive and flourish there must be very real faithfulness and what we might call 'loyal love'. The partners must be able to trust each other absolutely and if that trust is weakened then the chances are that the marriage itself is doomed. In an age where marriage is being downgraded and divorce and cohabitation is at an all time high the need to know and experience the work of the Holy Spirit is even greater. There is need to truly know His power in our lives that produces the fruit of faithfulness.

D. IN OUR SUFFERING: the greatest example of faithfulness in suffering was our Saviour, the Lord Jesus Christ. He was faithful unto death, being willing to die for our sins on the cross and for that loyalty to the Father's purpose we give thanks today. We are warned many times in Scripture that we will walk in the Saviour's footsteps and we too will know pain, suffering, temptations, opposition and trials. We are called upon to suffer. Jesus said, *"No servant is greater than his master. If they persecuted me, they will persecute you also"* (John 15:20, NIV). Also the apostle Paul wrote, *"Everyone who wants to live a godly life in Christ Jesus will be persecuted"* (2 Tim. 3:12, NIV). This was certainly true for the early church, where there were many believers imprisoned, beaten and even killed for their faith in Christ. Indeed the early church at Smyrna was specifically told that it would suffer but it was called to *"be faithful, even to the point of death, and I will give you the crown of life"* (Rev. 2:10, NIV). Death is the ultimate price of loyalty and the believer who is faithful unto death is promised the blessing of a crown in heaven. There is rich reward from God to His people who are faithful even under the most horrific conditions. We must ever be faithful and endure anything and everything for the sake of loyalty to the Lord Jesus. Let it be true of us that at the end we will be able to say the words that the apostle Paul could utter in his last epistle, *"I have fought the good fight, I have finished the race, I have kept the faith. Now there is in store for me the crown of righteousness, which the Lord, the righteous Judge, will award to me on that day—and not only to me, but also to all who have longed for his appearing"* (2 Tim. 4:7-8, NIV). It will be a wonderful blessing to hear the words of the Lord Jesus at the end of our work on earth, *"Well done, thou good and faithful servant...enter thou into the joy of thy lord"* (Matt. 25:21).

So we are called to be faithful in every area and part of our lives. It means being faithful to the people and the responsibilities God has given us. Let us today seek the powerful working of the Holy Spirit in our lives so that we might be faithful and serve the Lord with total loyalty for His glory.

Faithfulness in little things is a big thing.
Chrysostom

Meekness Not Weakness

Meekness is the mark of a man who has been
mastered by God.   *Geoffrey B. Wilson*

"The fruit of the Spirit is…meekness" (Gal. 5:23). The word
"meekness" carries the idea of gentle humility or a quiet spirit.
This should be a strong characteristic in each and every
Christian in our dealings with other people. Yet here we hit
a snag straightaway because many people equate meekness
with weakness and feel that the meek person is timid, spine-
less, feeble and lacks energy. Yet this is a caricature and is far
removed from the teaching of the New Testament. There we
see the rough, tough, impetuous fisherman known as Simon
Peter. He was far from weak and has been described by Lloyd
Douglas as "The Big Fisherman". This strong man gradually
learned to have his strength controlled and channelled by the
Holy Spirit.

MEEKNESS—DEFINITION

Jesus said, *"Blessed are the meek"* (Matt. 5:5) and the idea
of the word *"Blessed"* is to be radiantly happy or having a
quality which deserves congratulations or is to be envied.
So to possess the quality of meekness is a wonderful blessing. Yet so often that is the very last notion we would give
to the quality of being meek but meekness is a hard word
to define because "it is not readily expressed in English."[9].

---

9   W. E. Vine

It is a strong term in Scripture but also carries the idea of gentleness, humility or mildness. Essentially it is not living in a self-centred manner and is neither self-assertive nor self-seeking. Yet neither is it weakness as the old saying indicates, "meekness is not weakness". It is strength under control, strength that is channelled for the good of others. It is strength under authority.

One of the greatest Welsh soccer players of all time was John Charles. He was a big man who scored many goals and played to a very high standard. He never reacted violently or aggressively when fouled on the pitch and in those days there was much less protection from referees than there is today. Yet he played with power but kept his strength under control and was known as "the gentle giant".

In the Old Testament the great Israelite leader Moses was described as *"a very humble man, more humble than anyone else on the face of the earth"* (Num. 12:3, NIV). Clearly he was not weak. We know that in his early days he killed a man and so was clearly physically strong. Later he drove away shepherds so that a shepherdess (who would later be his wife) could water the flocks. He was strong and brave and later led the nation of Israel from Egypt to the Promised Land. He was their leader for forty years and that required a strength of character that was absolutely outstanding. Moses developed the right attitude towards God. He recognized the greatness of God and his absolute dependence upon Him. "Meekness is humility before God." His focus was upon the Lord, both His Word and His will. Also Moses developed a correct attitude to the people of Israel. He cared for their welfare, even though he had to put up with their criticism, opposition, complaining and grumbling. He kept going because he had their best interests at heart and did his best to protect them and care for them. Humble meekness is simply a willingness to do God's will but recognizing our own limitations and so seeking God's help to fulfil that will. We need meekness in two areas of life.

1. MEEKNESS TOWARDS GOD

Someone has said that meekness is "humility before God". It is recognizing our dependence upon God. Every day we receive an abundance of blessings from the Almighty, indeed we are dependent upon Him for our very next breath. He is the source of all mercy and we need Him. So we must show no arrogance in the presence of the Lord but meekly, humbly and gently bow before Him in worship, gratitude and praise. Most of all we praise Him for His grace that gave us the greatest of all gifts, namely His Son the Lord Jesus. We did not deserve the least gift from God but He was willing to give to mankind the greatest of all possible blessings. Such meekness was reflected in Moses who was not concerned to promote himself but was deeply concerned for the honour of God and the welfare of the Lord's people.

2. MEEKNESS TOWARDS PEOPLE

When we think of Moses we realize that he had an impetuous nature and he was more than capable of displaying bouts of hot temper and strong passion. On one occasion he killed an Egyptian (Ex. 2:12) and on another he struck the rock twice in anger (Num. 20:11). Yet these were occasional outbursts and he learnt during forty years as a shepherd in the desert to be habitually controlled by care and concern for others. That was wonderfully demonstrated when He led Israel out of Egypt. He was gentle to the people and had learnt to bring his strength under control.

So we see that meekness is power, strength, wildness but very much under control. Also implied is the idea of sensitivity. The horse that has been tamed has as much strength as when it was wild, but now it is under control and is very sensitive to its rider and moves and responds to a simple touch. Thus meekness is strength harnessed. Similarly the meek man may be just as strong as the violent man, but his strength is bridled by the Spirit of God. It was the human rights activist and Christian preacher Martin Luther King who said, "Christians should be tough minded and tender hearted."

THE MEEKNESS OF CHRIST

We are aware that because strength has been taken out of the concept of meekness the popular character of Jesus is grossly misrepresented. He is so often viewed as tepid, soft and sentimental. This is encouraged by singing "Gentle Jesus, Meek and Mild"[10] and by artists who so often portray Him as white, delicate and cuddling woolly lambs. They tend to emphasize the tenderness, gentleness and affectionate aspects of His character at the expense of His courage, active and sterner side. It certainly required strength and courage to stand up to the Pharisees of His day and to drive out traders and moneychangers from the Temple area.

The Lord was certainly meek because He said, *"I am meek and lowly in heart"* (Matt. 11:29). He was a gentle teacher, being patient with the slow and considerate to all including outcasts, children and women. Quietly He went about exercising a ministry of sympathy and encouragement and His strength lay in His meekness. We see this dual aspect of the Lord's nature in Revelation 5. In verse five the Lord is pictured as a lion and that reminds of His strength, majesty and power. He is the King. Yet in verse six He is pictured as a lamb and this reminds us of His sacrifice, when quietly and without protest He went to Calvary and died for our sins. He is the Saviour. Thus the strength of the lion was seen in the lamb. When He could have destroyed His enemies and tormentors He did not, instead He kept His power and authority under control. This was the strength of meekness when the Son of God was crucified for our sins. The lion is the lamb.

All Christian growth will include the development of a meek and gentle spirit and is seen as the Holy Spirit develops a spiritual poise and inward quietness. It is the opposite of pride. Pride is the result of looking inward and glorying in

---

10   Charles Wesley, Gentle Jesus, Meek and Mild

self, while meekness is the result of learning to look outward and upward and seeing the Lord Jesus. It is the result of seeking to live and walk under His authority and leading.

THE APPLICATION OF MEEKNESS

There are certain areas of life and particular circumstances where it is vitally important to show a meek and quiet spirit.

1. When our feelings are ruffled and we are upset. In those situations it is all too easy to react with violent defence and be aggressive to those who have upset us. Meekness does not react in this way but shows a quiet and peaceable spirit. This was a lesson that the apostle Peter had to learn. We remember that when a crowd came to arrest Jesus in the Garden of Gethsemane that Peter took out his sword and with violence cut off the ear of one of the arresting party. It was Jesus who told him to put away his sword and in an act of very great mercy healed that man who was injured. Later Peter was threatened, imprisoned and beaten but there was no reaction of violence but a willing submission to the will of God his Father. He eventually learnt to demonstrate meekness even in the face of the most appalling antagonism.

2. When we are not given the respect and position we feel that we deserve. There are people who crave preeminence and the chief place and one such person in the New Testament was Diotrephes (3 John 9). It seems that anyone who stood up to him was ejected from the church and he made sure that his word was law. Meekness does not react like that and anyway the meek person who knows the fruit of the Spirit does not seek pre-eminence. That position in the local church is reserved for Christ and for Christ alone.

3. When we are not highly regarded. There were two people named Jannes and Jambres who deeply opposed the authority of Moses and seemed to want that same

authority for themselves (2 Tim. 3:8). They were rejected by God and were also found to be corrupted by ambition. Meekness does not seek personal recognition or desire high regard. The aim of those who have the spirit of meekness is summarized by the apostle Paul, *"For by the grace given me I say to every one of you: Do not think of yourself more highly than you ought, but rather think of yourself with sober judgement, in accordance with the measure of faith God has given you…be devoted to one another in brotherly love"* (Rom. 12:3, 10, NIV).

For every Christian it is important that meekness operates in relationship with other people in two areas of life.

1. TOWARDS FELLOW BELIEVERS

This is especially true when a fellow Christian has fallen into sinful ways and needs to be restored from a backslidden situation. The attempt at restoration must be done with a spirit of meekness and not with any presumed sense of superiority or pride. It is so important that we have no harsh, hard judgmentalism in our heart, which could creep into our attitude and dealings with a brother or sister who needs to be restored to the Lord. It is vital to remember that any Christian can be caught off guard, slip up unintentionally, be surprised by sin and be overcome by evil. Sin is a powerful and compelling enemy and when a believer slips the more mature members of the church fellowship need to try and help restore the offender.

Correction must never aim at punishment but at restoration because we should all be saying, "there but for the grace of God go I!" Indeed the apostle Paul makes the very same point in Galatians 6:1 (ESV), *"Brothers, if anyone is caught in any transgression, you who are spiritual should restore him in a spirit of gentleness* (or with a spirit of meekness). *Keep watch on yourself, lest you too be tempted."* The last part has been rendered, "Look to yourself, repairman, lest you too be tempted." Certainly the attitude we show should be one of deep humbleness and love as the apostle wrote, *"Love is never glad when others go wrong"* (1 Cor. 13:6, MNT[11]). We must walk in the footsteps of the Saviour who ever wanted to restore the backslider, find the lost and bring salvation to all.

2. TOWARDS NON-CHRISTIANS

Meekness is not only vital in the recovery of the fallen but also in the winning of those who are outside the fellowship of Christ. The attitude of the Christian is vital in this respect. All too easily we can find ourselves speaking and behaving in a manner that causes people to be repelled from the gospel rather than be attracted to it. The story is told of a man who went out every Sunday morning to church and at the same time his neighbour would be dressed for the golf course and be setting out for a round of golf. The neighbour invariably asked the Christian whether he would like to join him in a round of golf. The reply was a definite "No" and some mention that it was the Lord's Day! Some months later the man said to the Christian, "I have asked you join me for golf twenty-five times, while you have not asked me once to join you in church, instead you condemned me for playing golf on the Lord's Day." What a tragic and wasted opportunity and how different it could have been if the attitude had been a reflection of the Saviour's.

Knowing that we possess the glorious truth of the gospel should never make us over-confident or overbearing and certainly should not make us dogmatic and aggressive in stating our convictions. Meekness demands that we listen with interest and respect to the other person and we must guard against demonstrating a sense of assumed superiority and we must not be patronizing. Certainly we should never be aggressive or belligerent but we must learn to be persuasive and loving towards others in a spirit of meekness, as the apostles Paul and Peter make clear in the New Testament.

---

11   *Dynamic Translation of the New Testament in Macedonian,* (Skopje, Republic of Macedonia: HBC Radosna Vest, 1999)

THE APOSTLE PAUL

"Do not repay anyone evil for evil. Be careful to do what is right in the eyes of everybody. If it is possible, as far as it depends on you, live at peace with everyone" (Rom. 12:17-18, NIV). It is so important to accept others even though their beliefs and standards may be different from ours. We must respect others and deal with them in a careful and caring way.

"...be ready to do whatever is good, to slander no one, to be peaceable and considerate, and to show true humility toward all men" (Titus 3:1-2, NIV). This means that we must not always insist upon our rights and be willing to compromise in the areas of what may rightfully be ours. This should help us to avoid quarrelling which can repel a potential convert to Christ. *"And the Lord's servant must not quarrel; instead, he must be kind to everyone, able to teach, not resentful. Those who oppose him he must gently instruct, in the hope that God will grant them repentance leading them to a knowledge of the truth"* (2 Tim. 2:24-25, NIV).

THE APOSTLE PETER

"But and if ye suffer for righteousness' sake, happy are ye: and be not afraid of their terror, neither be troubled; But sanctify the Lord God in your hearts: and be ready always to give an answer to every man that asketh you a reason of the hope that is in you with meekness and fear" (1 Pet. 3:14-15). Again we are instructed to show courtesy and respect to everyone in all circumstances of life.

Like the Lord Jesus the true Christian should show meekness and this will manifest itself in an intense interest and concern for everyone and will enable each to be dealt with in an appropriate manner. "As icebergs are melted by the sun's rays—so hard hearts melt under the meekness of Christians indued by the Spirit"[12].

Ultimately this is the triumph of the meek. Where force incites resistance, meekness conquers all. Indeed the Bible links meekness with power and so by the action of God the

---

12   Billy Graham

one leads to the other. The Psalmist wrote, *"A little while…the meek will inherit the land and enjoy great peace"* (Ps. 37:10-11, NIV). Again the prophet Zechariah wrote, *"Rejoice greatly, O Daughter of Zion! Shout, Daughter of Jerusalem! See, your king comes to you, righteous and having salvation, gentle and riding on a donkey, on a colt, the foal of a donkey. I will take away the chariots from Ephraim and the war-horses from Jerusalem, and the battle-bow will be broken. He will proclaim peace to the nations. His rule will extend from sea to sea and from the River to the ends of the earth"* (Zech. 9:9-10, NIV). Here the instruments of violence are broken by meekness. The Messiah has overcome His enemy by way of the cross. The Lamb has triumphed and with Him those who are meek, the gentle strong shall inherit the earth. Let each one of us learn meekness and live for the glory of God.

> The meek man is not a human mouse afflicted with a sense of his own inferiority. Rather, he may be in his moral life as bold as a lion and as strong as Samson; but he has stopped being fooled by himself. He has accepted God's estimate of his own life. He knows he is weak and helpless as God has declared him to be, but paradoxically, he knows at the same time that he is, in the sight of God, more important than angels.   *A. W. Tozer*

Total Self-Control

> O God, help us to be masters of ourselves that
> we may be servants to others.
>
> *Sir Alec Paterson*

"The fruit of the Spirit is…self-control" (Gal. 5:23, NIV). Christians need to develop the characteristic of self-control. The word *"self-control"* has been translated as "temperance" but that word has in the past been closely associated with an anti-alcohol movement known as "The Temperance League". In its day it was highly commendable, as there was dreadful abuse of alcohol which impoverished families and induced terrible violence. Yet the idea of this characteristic that the Holy Spirit produces is not simply restricted to controlling the consumption of alcohol. It means having the mastery or control in all areas of life including thoughts, words and actions.

Someone has written, "There are men who can command armies, but cannot command themselves. There are men who by their burning words can sway vast multitudes who cannot keep silence under provocation and wrong. The highest mark of nobility is self-control. It is more kingly than regal crown and purple robe." Certainly such words are absolutely true and self-control should be the hallmark of the true Christian.

PAUL'S ATHLETE

The apostle Paul focused upon self-control in terms of the athlete training for a race and so he wrote, *"Do you not know that in a race all the runners run, but only one gets the prize? Run in such a way as to get the prize. Everyone who competes in the games goes into strict training. They do it to get a crown that will not last; but we do it to get a crown that will last forever. Therefore I do not run like a man running aimlessly; I do not fight like a man beating the air. No, I beat my body and make it my slave so that after I have preached to others, I myself will not be disqualified for the prize"* (1 Cor. 9:24-27, NIV). We notice five things from this statement of the apostle's,

1. The purpose is to run the race and for the Christian this means being spiritually fit for God's service.

2. To do well in the race there must be strict training and rigid discipline. Every athlete practices all round self-restraint. So every Christian should practice self-discipline.

3. It is the body that is controlled and mastered and that also applies to the Christian.

4. Everything is put into the training and the contest and nothing is left in reserve. So the Christian life is one of total involvement and complete commitment.

5. The prize in an athletic event was a crown of leaves but in the Christian race it is a crown of life.

Notice that Paul talked of the body being controlled and disciplined. In the Christian context this does not only mean the physical part of our lives but actually the totality of what we are. It is the whole person that is involved. The heart, mind, feelings, motives, words and actions are all involved. Clearly discipline in the outer areas of life depends upon discipline in the inner areas of life. There is no part of our person that does not need self-control. This is because we have been invaded by sin and any part of our being can be used as a base to attack the soul. For example our instincts and appetites make demands upon us and if they are uncontrolled then they become dangerous and destructive. Yet in themselves they are not evil. Thus a Christian is Christ's athlete who controls and consecrates all the powers of personal human nature to the glory of God. He does not root out or disown the various parts of his person but seeks to control them and exercise discipline over them.

ALL ROUND SELF-CONTROL

We notice too that it should be an all round self-control. This is because it is so easy to just concentrate upon one narrow aspect of life and ignore other areas of equal or even greater importance. It may be that we are self-controlled in the area of anger and do not lose our temper and we take great pride in our patience, especially when we see others being short-tempered. However, perhaps we forget that we are lazy and don't get up when we should, eat to excess and don't control our appetite or fail to control our tongues and are given to the most terrible gossip. Thus in our personal life it is too easy to be narrowly defined.

Discipline is distorted if we are over strict in some areas and over indulgent in others. This distortion needs to be corrected by recognition that we need an all-round discipline. We should not have an Achilles heel that could potentially destroy us. The hymn writer Charles Wesley wrote, "leave no unguarded place"[13].

Self-control is also about the idea of moderation. However, if a thing is inherently wrong (murder, stealing) then it cannot be right to do it all, even in strict moderation! Also there are some virtues (caring, giving) which should be carried out to excess. Yet there are other areas of life where moderation provides a very useful guideline and that is especially seen in the area of appetites. We can now look at three particular areas of life where self-control needs to be exercised.

WORK

If we are to know a healthy and satisfying life then both rest and work are vitally important. Yet it is possible that either rest or work can be carried to excess instead of being

---

13   Charles Wesley, *Soldiers of Christ, Arise*

moderated. Some have a constant desire for bodily rest and sleep. Such an approach is highlighted in the Old Testament in the following words, *"Go to the ant, you sluggard; consider its ways and be wise! It has no commander, no overseer or ruler, yet it stores its provisions in summer and gathers its food at harvest. How long will you lie there, you sluggard? When will you get up from your sleep? A little sleep, a little slumber, a little folding of the hands to rest—and poverty will come on you like a bandit and scarcity like an armed man"* (Prov. 6:6-11, NIV). This can be a strong warning for many in modern times where the wealthy societies have enabled some people to be idle and still have income. The welfare state should always be there for those who are genuinely ill and unable to work but should not reinforce the temptation to idleness. Clearly the Bible says that idleness is not good either for the health of the individuals concerned or for society as a whole.

However at the other extreme are those who work to excess. These are people who are workaholics. They have become emotionally dependent upon work not only for their livelihood but also for security, self-esteem and status. For them work has become a sort of drug and again this very much seems to be a modern, Western problem as people develop the drive for ever increasingly opulent lifestyles. Some people have even found it impossible to retire and seem utterly lost without the regular framework of their occupation.

The best example of someone who balanced these two ends of the spectrum was the Lord Jesus. He took time out from a busy schedule to rest, pray and recover His energy. Also there was no sense of frantic activity but a calm measured approach that focused upon and prioritized the important matters that had to be dealt with. So we see the need to be moderate both in our inactivity and sleep and our activity and work.

FOOD AND DRINK

It was Billy Graham who once wrote that, "Compulsive over eating is one of the most accepted and practiced sins of modern Western Christians." The problem is that gluttony perverts the natural function by making the pleasurable sensations which normally accompany eating an end in themselves. Over-eating can have serious physical repercussions and there is great concern in Western society with obesity and associated problems, especially in the young. Over eating can leave the mind feeling dull and heavy and the personality insensitive and unaware. Spiritually it can make us unable to truly worship and serve God. It is really using food as a drug and we even talk of "comfort eating" where it becomes a solace to take food when we feel down in our spirits. Someone has wisely said, "always rise from the table feeling that you would like a little more." Certainly to help control and discipline the intake of food the Bible urges the people of God to fast and to deny themselves the pleasure and distraction of eating for a period of time.

As well as too much food the Bible also condemns drunkenness. In fact the writer of the Proverbs became lyrical as he described the negative effect of too much drink. He wrote, *"Who has woe? Who has sorrow? Who has strife? Who has complaints? Who has needless bruises? Who has bloodshot eyes? Those who linger over wine, who go to sample bowls of mixed wine. Do not gaze at wine when it is red, when it sparkles in the cup, when it goes down smoothly! In the end it bites like a snake and poisons like a viper"* (Prov. 23:29-32, NIV). In the New Testament we read, *"Do not get drunk on wine, which leads to debauchery"* (Eph. 5:18, NIV).

The temperance movement encouraged people to sign a pledge for total abstinence and they had good reasons for doing so. They saw the devastating effects of drink on family life, the poverty it created and the neglect of children which it caused. They also saw that taking alcohol could lead many people on the downward path to addiction and today that is seen in the tens of thousand of alcoholics in our society. Drunken driving maims and kills many people, while drink clearly lowers people resistance to temptation in both the sexual and violent areas of life. Also it can also be seen as a colossal waste of money when so many people are starving in our world today. Many Christians as a consequence have become teetotal or total abstainers from alcohol as a result of these problems.

However we might decide that the need is not for total abstinence but total moderation. We do have freedom and we must make up our own minds and decide for ourselves before the Lord. Certainly if we are to enjoy alcohol we must enjoy it in moderation and must appreciate that there may be weaker Christians who do not have the same freedom and might be offended. We should all respect the convictions of others who may have different views from ourselves. So whether abstinence or moderation let all learn to be caring towards those who may act differently.

THE TONGUE

In James 3:8 we read, *"No man can tame the tongue. It is a restless evil, full of deadly poison"* (NIV). This reminds us that words are powerful and can deeply affect people. The little tongue can be used to wound, hurt and destroy people it can be a powerful force for evil, but it can also be used to praise God and preach the gospel and so can be a powerful force for spiritual good. However too often it can create havoc and hurt and we must guard against misuse of words. The following are to be guarded against.

THE SINS OF SPEECH

A. LYING: when we lie and deceive people it produces distrust and destroys fellowship. We are commanded in the New Testament to *"put off falsehood and speak truthfully"* (Eph. 4:25, NIV).

B. DIRTY TALK: this means foul language that pollutes and defiles both speaker and hearer. Again we are instructed, *"Do not let any unwholesome talk come out of your mouths"* (Eph. 4:29, NIV).

C. INSULTING AND ABUSIVE LANGUAGE: this can

so often spring from anger and contempt and needs to be avoided. Jesus said, *"Anyone who is angry with his brother will be subject to judgment"* (Matt. 5:22, NIV).

D. SLANDER: this is essentially character assassination committed by gossips and scandalmongers. They harm reputations as they speak about people behind their backs. Slander always produces three victims, firstly the slanderer, secondly the hearer and thirdly the person being slandered.

Certainly if the tongue is ever to be tamed then it must be by the Holy Spirit because no man can tame it. We can use three steps to help in the process of controlling the misuse of our tongue.

A. STOP AND THINK: we need to remember that there is great potential in words and realize that they can be both a blessing and a curse. We need to constantly make Psalm 141:3 our prayer, *"Set a guard over my mouth, O Lord; keep watch over the door of my lips"* (NIV).

B. SPEAK THE TRUTH: the Psalmist talks of the person *"who speaks the truth from his heart"* (Ps. 15:2, NIV). Everything we say should be tested as to whether it is true. It is not sufficient to avoid the deliberate lie, but also false impressions should be avoided due to exaggeration, distortion, withholding of facts and quoting out of context. We must be sure to speak the truth.

C. SPEAK THE TRUTH IN LOVE: this is what the apostle Paul said in Ephesians 4:15, *"speaking the truth in love"* (NIV). It is obviously possible to speak the truth in an unkind and hurtful manner. There is a place for constructive criticism but we must be careful when and how we give it. Certainly to be brutally frank can cause all manner of hurt and dislocation in someone's life. We need very much to be self-controlled in our speech.

It is important to exercise self-control in all areas of life. There are so many parts where we can fail and we need to be constantly dependent upon the Lord to sustain us in the midst of difficult times. Such areas are:

A. DEFEAT: when we have failed, been defeated and faced setbacks it is easy to lose hope and give up. Somehow in Christ we must sustain hope.

B. SEXUAL MATTERS: there should be abstinence in sexual matters before marriage and total fidelity within marriage.

C. THOUGHTS: we should be very careful not to develop wrong mental habits and so we should be self-controlled as to what we watch, listen to or read. We must do our utmost in prayerful dependence upon the Lord to break up bad mental habits.

We live in a time when violence, selfishness and undisciplined living threaten to destroy the planet. It is imperative and vitally important that as Christian believers we set an example in self-controlled living through the power of the indwelling Spirit of God.

No man is free who cannot command himself.

Pythagoras

Also by Paul Young

The Bitter Spirit: The Deadly Effects of Bitterness*

Bitterness is a deeply destructive emotion.

It can develop in our spirits like infection in a physical wound. It can make us ineffective and useless for God's service and could undermine the work of our church and its standing in our community. A bitter reaction will always undermine the integrity of the Gospel because the Gospel is a message that conquers bitterness.

The Lord Jesus took all our bitterness on the cross where the ultimate price for sin was paid by Him. So in Christ we can find release from the oppressive bondage that bitterness produces. May God grant us the grace to always leave bitterness at the feet of the Saviour so that we can live life unburdened by the weight of a bitter spirit which ultimately will cause the most damage to ourselves.

The End of a Nation: Studies of Obadiah*

The Friend Abraham and the Promise of God Isaac*

Understanding the Bible*
Inspiration, Inerrancy & Interpretation

Outreach Through the Local Church
Problems and needs

The New Age Movement: A Cunningly Devised Fable*
A detailed look at this movement

Raging Waves: Studies in the Epistle of Jude

*Cunningly Devised Fables**
   A look at 13 cults and religions and an overview of
   their characteristics

The Challenge of Revival
   A look back at the 1904 Welsh Revival and a challenge
   for us in the present

The Diary of a Prophet
   Studies in the book of Haggai

A Glimmer of Light
   Studies in the book of Lamentations

All books available from:
31, Fairmeadows, Maesteg, South Wales, CF34 9JL

*Books available from **GOSPEL FOLIO PRESS**
www.gospelfolio.com • (905)-835-9166